PASSING THE UNITED NATIONS NATIONAL COMPETITIVE RECRUITMENT EXAMINATION (YOUNG PROFESSIONALS PROGRAMME EXAM)

Legal Affairs Occupational Group

JuraLaw

Passing the United Nations National Competitive Recruitment Examination
(Young Professionals Programme Exam):
Legal Affairs Occupational Group

2016 Edition

ISBN (13) (paperback): 978-1-68109-078-8
ISBN (10) (paperback): 1-68109-078-3
ISBN (13) (Kindle): 978-1-68109-079-5
ISBN (10) (Kindle): 1-68109-079-1

JuraLaw

JuraLaw™
an imprint of TellerBooks™
TellerBooks.com/Time_Books

TellerBooks

www.TellerBooks.com/JuraLaw

Professional Examination Success Guides

Passing the Uniform Bar Exam:
Outlines and Cases to Help You Pass the Bar in New York and Twenty-Three Other States

Passing the United Nations National Competitive Recruitment Examination
(Young Professionals Programme Exam)
Legal Affairs Occupational Group

TABLE OF CONTENTS

ABBREVIATIONS

Where appropriate, acronyms correspond to the names of treaties as they are commonly known (*e.g.*, "MT" for Moon Treaty), rather than by the full treaty title.

ACHR......................... American Convention on Human Rights (1969)

ADRDM..................... American Declaration of the Rights and Duties of Man (1948)

APM.......................... Anti-Personnel Mine

ATCA........................ Alien Tort Claims Act (28 USC 1350)

ATS .... Antarctic Treaty System (Antarctic Treaty and related agreements) (1961)

AU .... African Union

CBU .... cluster bomb unit

CC .... Chicago Convention on International Civil Aviation (1944) (Chicago Convention)

CCW.......................... UN Convention on Prohibitions or Restrictions on the Use of Certain Conventional Weapons Which May be Deemed to be Excessively Injurious or to Have Indiscriminate Effects (Geneva, 1980)

CDHRI .... Cairo Declaration on Human Rights in Islam

CDR .... Cartagena Declaration on Refugees

COE........................... Council of Europe

CEDAW .... The Convention on the Elimination of all Forms of Discrimination against Women

CERD......................... Committee on the Elimination of Racial Discrimination

CFC .... chlorofluorocarbon

CFREU...................... The Charter of Fundamental Rights of the European Union (2000)

COAS......................... Charter of the Organization of American States (1967)

CPHR .... European Convention for the Protection of Human Rights and Fundamental Freedoms (European Convention on Human Rights)

CPPG......................... Convention on the Prevention and Punishment of the Crime of Genocide (Genocide Convention) (1948)

CRC........................... Committee on the Rights of the Child

CRSR .... Convention Relating to the Status of Refugees (1951)

CUN .... Charter of the United Nations (1945)

DARS........................ Draft Articles on the Responsibility of States for Internationally Wrongful Acts (2001) (Draft Articles on State Responsibility) (ILC document)

ECHR......................... European Court of Human Rights

ECJ............................ European Court of Justice

ECOSOC.................... Economic and Social Council

EU .... European Union

GA............................. General Assembly (of the UN)

GATT .... General Agreement on Tariffs and Trade

GC I............................Geneva Convention (I) for the Amelioration of the Condition of the Wounded and Sick in Armed Forces in the Field (1949)

GC II ....Geneva Convention (II) for the Amelioration of the Condition of Wounded, Sick and Shipwrecked Members of Armed Forces at Sea (1949)

GC III........................Geneva Convention (III) relative to the Treatment of Prisoners of War. Geneva (1949)

GC IV........................Geneva Convention (IV) relative to the Protection of Civilian Persons in Time of War. Geneva (1949)

GCTS ....Geneva Convention on the Territorial Sea and Contiguous Zone

HC IV........................Hague Convention (IV) respecting the Laws and Customs of War on Land and its annex: Regulations concerning the Laws and Customs of War on Land (1907)

HCPIL ....Hague Conference on Private International Law

HRC ....Human Rights Committee (of the ICCPR)

IACHR.......................Inter-American Commission on Human Rights

IACtHR......................Inter-American Court of Human Rights

ICAO.........................International Civil Aviation Organization

ICC............................International Criminal Court

ICCPR.......................International Covenant on Civil and Political Rights

ICERD.......................International Convention on the Elimination of All Forms of Racial Discrimination

ICESCR.....................International Covenant on Economic, Social and Cultural Rights

ICJ.............................International Court of Justice

ICRC ....International Committee of the Red Cross

ICTR ....International Criminal Tribunal for Rwanda

ICTY ....International Criminal Tribunal for the former Yugoslavia

IHL............................International humanitarian law

ILC ....International Law Commission

ILO............................International Labor Organization

IMT ....International Military Tribunal (Nuremberg)

IMTFE.......................International Military Tribunal for the Far East

ISA ....International Seabed Authority

ITLS ....International Tribunal for the Law of the Sea

ITO............................International Trade Organization

LC ....Charter of the International Military Tribunal (London Charter) (1945)

MBT..........................Ottawa Convention on the Prohibition of the Use, Stockpiling, Production and Transfer of Anti-Personnel Mines and on their Destruction (Mine Ban Treaty)

MT.............................Agreement Governing the Activities of States on the Moon and Other Celestial Bodies (1979) (Moon Treaty)

NAT ....North Atlantic Treaty

NATO ....North Atlantic Treaty Organization

NGO..........................Non-governmental organization

OAS...........................Organization of American States

OAU..........................Organisation of African Unity

OIC .... Organisation of the Islamic Conference
OST .... Treaty on principles governing the activities of states in the exploration and use of outer space, including the moon and other celestial bodies (1967) (Outer Space Treaty)
PCT .... Patent Cooperation Treaty (1970)
PRC .... People's Republic of China
RC .... Republic of China
RFR .... Restatement 3d of the Foreign Relations Law of the U.S.
§ .... Section
SC .... Security Council (of the UN)
SCSL .... Special Court for Sierra Leone
SDR .... Special Drawing Rights
SICC .... Rome Statute of the International Criminal Court
SICJ .... Statute of the International Court of Justice
STL .... Special Tribunal for Lebanon
TC .... Trusteeship Council
UDHR .... Universal Declaration of Human Rights (1948)
UN .... United Nations
UNCED .... United Nations Conference on Environment and Development (Earth Summit)
UNCHR .... United Nations Commission on Human Rights (ECOSOC subsidiary)
UNCITRAL .... United Nations Commission on International Trade Law
UNCLOS .... United Nations Convention on the Law of the Sea (1982)
UNCLOS I .... First United Nations Conference on the Law of the Sea (1958)
UNCLOS II .... Second United Nations Conference on the Law of the Sea (1960)
UNCLOS III .... Third United Nations Conference on the Law of the Sea (1982)
UNCRC .... UN Convention on the Rights of the Child (1989)
UNEP .... United Nations Environment Programme
UNFCCC .... UN Framework Convention on Climate Change (1992)
UNHCHR .... Office of the United Nations High Commissioner for Human Rights
UNHCR .... Office of the United Nations High Commissioner for Refugees
UNHRC .... UN Human Rights Council
UNIDROIT .... International Institute for the Unification of Private Law
UNS .... United Nations Secretariat
US .... United States of America
USC .... United States Code
USPTO .... US Patent and Trademark Office
USSR .... Union of Soviet Socialist Republics
VCDR .... Vienna Convention on Diplomatic Relations (1961)
VCLT .... Vienna Convention on the Law of Treaties (1969)
WCED .... World Commission on Environment and Development
WIPO .... World Intellectual Property Organization
WSSD .... World Summit on Sustainable Development (2002)
WTO .... World Trade Organization
WWII .... World War II

TABLE OF INTERNATIONAL INSTRUMENTS

These treaties and other international instruments are listed according to the year in which they were concluded and opened for signature—not necessarily the year in which they entered into force. They are listed according to the name or acronym by which they are commonly known.

1963..........Treaty Banning Nuclear Weapon Tests in the Atmosphere, in Outer Space and Under Water (also known as the Nuclear Test Ban Treaty)

1966..........International Covenant on Economic, Social and Cultural Rights, 16 December 1966 (entry into force 3 January 1976)

1966..........International Covenant on Civil and Political Rights, 16 December 1966 (entry into force 23 March 1976)

1966..........International Convention on the Elimination of All Forms of Racial Discrimination

1967..........Charter of the Organization of American States

1967..........Treaty on principles governing the activities of states in the exploration and use of outer space, including the moon and other celestial bodies (Outer Space Treaty)

1967..........Protocol Relating to the Status of Refugees

1969..........American Convention on Human Rights (Pact of San José)

1969..........Vienna Convention on the Law of Treaties

1970..........Patent Cooperation Treaty, done at Washington on June 19, 1970

1977..........Protocol Additional to the Geneva Conventions of 12 August 1949, and relating to the Protection of Victims of International Armed Conflicts (Protocol I), 8 June 1977 (entry into force 7 December 1979)

1977..........Protocol Additional to the Geneva Conventions of 12 August 1949, and relating to the Protection of Victims of Non-International Armed Conflicts (Protocol II), 8 June 1977 (entry into force 7 December 1979)

1979..........Agreement Governing the Activities of States on the Moon and Other Celestial Bodies (Moon Treaty)

1979..........Convention on the Elimination of All Forms of Discrimination Against Women

1980..........UN Convention on Prohibitions or Restrictions on the Use of Certain Conventional Weapons Which May be Deemed to be Excessively Injurious or to Have Indiscriminate Effects

1981..........African Charter on Human and Peoples' Rights

1982..........UN Convention on the Law of the Sea

1989..........Indigenous and Tribal Peoples Convention

1989..........UN Convention on the Rights of the Child

1992..........UN Framework Convention on Climate Change

1993..........Convention on the Prohibition of the Development, Production, Stockpiling and Use of Chemical Weapons and on their Destruction

1994..........General Agreement on Tariffs and Trade

1996..........Comprehensive Nuclear Test Ban Treaty

1997..........Ottawa Convention on the Prohibition of the Use, Stockpiling, Production and Transfer of Anti-Personnel Mines and on their Destruction (Mine Ban Treaty)

1998..........Statute of the International Criminal Court (Rome Statute) (entry into force 2002)

1999..........Convention for the Unification of Certain Rules for International Carriage (Montreal Convention)

2000..........The Charter of Fundamental Rights of the European Union

2005..........Protocol additional to the Geneva Conventions of 12 August 1949, and relating to the Adoption of an Additional Distinctive Emblem (Protocol III), 8 December 2005 (entry into force 14 January 2006)

TABLE OF ICJ CASES

1949......... *Albania v. Great Britain* (Corfu Channel case) (1949) –Albania was ordered to compensate Britain for damage caused by Albania's mining of the channel.

1981......... *Canada v. United States* (Delimitation of the Maritime Boundary in the Gulf of Maine Area).

1982......... *United States v. Iran* ("US Diplomatic and Consular Staff in Tehran case") – states are responsible for the conduct of non-state actors if they subsequently ratify the conduct and adopt it as their own.

1984......... *The Republic of Nicaragua v. The United States of America* – by supporting Contra guerrillas in their rebellion against the Nicaraguan government, the US had violated "its obligations under customary international law not to use force against another State," "not to intervene in its affairs," "not to violate its sovereignty," "not to interrupt peaceful maritime commerce," and "its obligations under Article XIX of the Treaty of Friendship, Commerce and Navigation between the Parties signed at Managua on 21 January 1956."

1985......... *Libyan Arab Jamahiriya v. Malta* ("Continental Shelf case") – state practice, together with the *opinio juris* of states, forms the substance of customary law.

1995......... *New Zealand v. France* ("Nuclear Tests Case").

1998......... *Libyan Arab Jamahiriya v. United States of America* ("Lockerbie Case").

1999......... *Botswana v. Namibia* – territorial dispute case in which the ICJ ruled in favor of Botswana's claim over Sedudu Island.

1999......... *Yugoslavia v. Belgium* (Legality of the Use of Force Application of the Federal Republic of Yugoslavia) – for the ICJ to have jurisdiction over the case, Yugoslavia would have had to have accepted compulsory jurisdiction under article 36(2) SICJ prior to the occurrence of the events.

2004......... *Mexico v. United States* (Case Concerning Avena and other Mexican Nationals) – the US was found to be in breach of the VCDR for failing to inform certain Mexican nationals imprisoned in the US of their right to contact their embassy and was required to review all sentences of the nationals.

2007......... *Bosnia and Herzegovina v. Serbia and Montenegro* (Application of the Convention on the Prevention and Punishment of the Crime of Genocide) – Belgrade breached international law by failing to prevent the 1995 Srebrenica genocide and for failing to try or transfer the persons accused of genocide to the ICTY.

2010......... *ICJ advisory opinion on Kosovo's declaration of independence* – declared that Kosovo's unilateral declaration of independence did not violate international law.

CHAPTER 1. QUESTIONS ASKED IN PREVIOUS TEST ADMINISTRATIONS

I. NATIONAL COMPETITIVE RECRUITMENT EXAMINATION – UN SECRETARIAT LEGAL AFFAIRS OCCUPATIONAL GROUP

The following section is based on questions that were asked in an actual administration of the National Competitive Recruitment Examination.

* * *

Of the following five cases, choose four and present an analysis under applicable public international law.

A. The Law of War and Armed Conflict and the International Recognition of States

Sporadic outbreaks of violence in a Sub-Saharan African country eventually escalate into a full-blown civil war. During this war, a government defense minister, acting on his own and without specific orders from the country's president or parliament, led a massacre against an ethnic minority living in one of the nation's provinces. At the conclusion of the war, the province declared independence and was recognized by eleven States in the international community.

What laws apply to the acts of the defense minister and in what ways can he be held accountable for his crimes?

B. UN Immunity and International Contract Law

The United Nations entered into an agreement with an independent contractor for the delivery of generators in a State where the United Nations was working. The contractor breached the terms of the contract because through a late delivery. Customs duties were imposed on the UN at the port of entry at the time of the delivery of the generators.

What recourse does the United Nations have at its disposal in order to recover its losses from breach of contract and challenge the imposition of duties?

C. Treaty Law

You are the legal advisor of a United Nations member State. The State wishes to enter into a multilateral treaty, but has reservations with respect to one of the articles. Nothing in the treaty speaks about whether countries could make reservations or amend the treaty. You were asked to advise the State as to what it should do, giving special attention to the Vienna Convention on the Law of Treaties and the Vienna Convention on the Law of Treaties between States and International Organizations or between International Organizations.

D. International Trade Law

A company wishes to enter into international markets and you are to advise its management on the various international legal instruments that could be used to promote its commerce overseas. Given special attention to the General Agreement on Tariffs and Trade, the World Trade Organization and the various international conventions protecting intellectual and industrial property.

E. Law of the Sea

Several States, including a landlocked country, are using the territorial waters and exclusive economic zones of coastal and archipelagic States for the purpose of trade and the disposal of waste. Discuss the rights and duties of each State vis-à-vis the other States, with special focus on those States that signed the 1982 United Nations Convention on the Law of the Sea as well as customary law that binds States that have not signed the Convention.

II. UNITED NATIONS SECRETARIAT ORAL EXAMINATION

The following section is based on questions that were asked in an actual oral exam administered by the UN Secretariat.

*   *   *

A. UN Competencies Test: Tips

The following are useful tips to bear in mind while preparing for your interview:

1. Prepare a **wide range of brief real life stories** about your accomplishments. Be aware of the specific skills each story illustrates and remember to include the positive outcome or lesson learned from each experience.

2. Be ready to discuss your strengths and your ability to learn from past experiences. Also think about how you could contribute to the work of the United Nations and to the specific position you are applying for.

3. Review the **competencies** mentioned in the job opening. These will be probed in your interview, so your stories should show your skill in these competency areas.

4. You should be prepared to address positive results and achievements using these competencies and also challenges you have had in each of these areas.

5. The structure of your answer should be: **Situation, Action, Result**.

6. Share information you feel is appropriate and relevant.

7. **Listen to the question carefully. Keep to the point. Be as specific as possible**.

8. Do some research on **competency, or behavior based interviews**. There is a lot of material available about preparing for such an interview structure.

9. Learn as much as you can about the Department and Office you are applying to and the work it does.

B. UN Competencies Test: Sample Questions

1. Give an example of when you had an interpersonal conflict in a team and how you resolved it.

2. Who do you consider your client?

3. Give an example of when you served your client that went positively. Explain what was asked for, what you gave them, and how it went.

4. Give an example of when you served your client that went negatively. Explain what was asked for, what you gave them, and how it went.

5. How have you dealt with interpersonal conflict in a multicultural setting?

6. Give an example of when you had missed a deadline. What did you do?

7. How do you handle various competing priorities?

C. Substantive, Knowledge-Based Questions: Overview

This section of the oral exam tests general knowledge of the United Nations and international affairs. Topics in which the questions may fall include the following:
(i) the United Nations;
(ii) science and the environment;
(iii) development and human rights; and
(iv) international politics.

For each topic, you will pick a number at random and the panel will select a question.

D. Substantive, Knowledge-Based Questions: Sample Questions

The following questions are taken from an actual oral interview administered by the United Nations Secretariat:

1. What challenges does the United Nations currently face in achieving its mission?

2. Discuss the composition of the Security Council and moves to reform it.

3. Discuss the internet and its impact on connections between people.

4. Define child soldiers and discuss efforts to protect children from becoming child soldiers.

5. Define economic sanctions and give two examples of their imposition.

6. Discuss some of the challenges to the application and enforcement of international humanitarian law in modern warfare.

III. SPECIAL TRIBUNAL FOR LEBANON WRITTEN EXAMINATION

The following questions were asked in a previous administration of the Special Tribunal for Lebanon's written examination:

* * *

Instructions: Please respond to question 1 in English and question 2 in French within 2 hours.

Question 1: As part of the evidence against the accused at the STL, an expert report analysing communications allegedly made between the accused and other persons prior to and on the day of the attack against the Prime Minister Rafik Hariri has been disclosed to the defence. The defence wishes to challenge the admissibility into evidence of this report and asks you to draft a brief memo identifying grounds to that aim. Please do so.

Question 2 : Pourquoi est-il important d'avoir un Bureau de la Défense, organe indépendant, au sein d'un tribunal pénal international?

IV. UNRWA WRITTEN AND ORAL EXAMINATIONS

A. UNRWA Oral Examination: Round I

The following questions were asked in a previous administration of an UNRWA oral exam.

* * *

1. What do you know about UNRWA and what is your motivation in applying?

2. Explain a time when you had to negotiate a complex contractual transaction.

3. Explain a time when you worked in a team and it went well and why.

4. Explain a time where you worked in a team and it went poorly and why.

5. Have you had someone that you do not get along with and how did you handle the situation?

6. The Director of UNRWA is interested in receiving a gift of $500,000 from an Arab Sheikh, but wants to avoid entering a warranty in the agreement whereby the Sheikh warrants that the funds have no terrorist origins because the Director does not wish to offend the Sheikh. What would you tell the Director and why?

7. How do you prioritize competing tasks?

B. UNRWA Oral Examination: Round II

The following questions were asked in a previous second-round UNRWA oral exam.

* * *

1. What do you foresee as your work in UNRWA and what do you consider to be most rewarding?

2. What is the biggest problem that you had to handle in the last 6 months?

3. What was some urgent advice that you had to provide on very short notice for a client? How was the advice transmitted?

4. Give an example of where you had to communicate some very complex information to a client. How were you able to communicate it? Was the client satisfied?

5. It is Christmas break and you are the only lawyer in the office. The director of the Jordan office calls and informs you that a cashier has just taken $200,000 and is leaving because he is tired of waiting for the early retirement funds that were promised to him. These funds equal about $200,000. The money taken came out of a $500,000 special fund for Syrian refugees. What do you do?

6. How would your answer change if you later found out that that this is an employee that has had a clean 20-year employment record, that he has been waiting an inordinate amount of time for his early retirement payment, that the amount he took was equal to what was owed? The head of human resources asked whether we could just let him keep the money as what is owed to him by giving approval to his $200,000, which has been lagging.

7. Give an example of when you had to be a part of making strategic or policy decisions.

8. What is a case where a client asked you to do something that you did not think you could deliver? How did you handle the situation?

CHAPTER 2. PUBLIC INTERNATIONAL LAW OUTLINE

I. INTRODUCTION

A. The Definition and Origins of International Law

International Law can be defined as the set of binding rules and principles that govern the relations and dealings of nations and international organizations with one another and with natural or juridical persons. The Restatement 3d of the Foreign Relations Law of the U.S. thus states that international law "consists of rules and principles of general application dealing with the conduct of states and of international organizations and with their relations *inter se*, as well as with some of their relations with persons, whether natural or juridical" (§ 101 RFR).

International law can be said to have begun with the Dutch jurist Hugo Grotius (1583-1645), whose writings established the basis of international law based on natural law, as well as with the Peace of Westphalia of 1648, which put an end to the Thirty Years War in the Holy Roman Empire and the Eighty Years' War (1568–1648) between Spain and the Dutch Republic and gave rise to the birth of modern nation states, which looked to the new development of international law to govern the relationships and conduct among each another.

B. Public versus Private International Law

Public international law concerns itself with questions of rights between several nations and some questions of rights between nations and the citizens or subjects of other nations. Private international law, in contrast, governs the activities of and relations between natural and juridical persons when they cross national borders. Private international law involves such areas as trade and commerce, finance and banking, trusts and estates, and family law matters, including international child abduction between private litigants when a foreign element is present. In these cases, conflict of law provisions must be invoked in order to determine (i) which jurisdictions have competence to hear a case; and (ii) the laws of which jurisdiction are to be applied by the court hearing the case.

According to Anthony Aust, the major difference between public and private international law is that while public international law seeks to layout a regime of supernational norms that govern issues having foreign elements, private international law is a body of domestic legal rules that are used to determine which laws should be applied when such a case having foreign elements arises. While true (public) international law is a system of positive international legal instruments, private international law is merely domestic *conflict of laws*. Thus, organizations such as HCPIL, UNIDROIT, and UNCITRAL that seek to harmonize states' domestic laws in a variety of areas ranging from conflict of laws to international trade law fall within private international law (conflict of laws), and organizations such as the WTO that write international laws binding on member states fall within public international law, as they do not deal with states' domestic laws strictly speaking.

Public international law, which is often referred to simply as "international law," is the main subject of this treatise. Private international law will only be mentioned in passing.

C. Subjects of International Law

1. Overview

The subjects of international law are thus (i) states; (ii) international organizations; (iii) juridical persons; and (iv) natural persons. All of these subjects bear the rights and responsibilities of international law.

States are the primary subjects of international law. International law developed to regulate states as a result of state interaction, particularly in times of war. The laws of war developed because of the mutual interests of all states to regulate the use of force in wartime and to create a legal framework that will make the emergence of war less likely.

Both natural and juridical persons are also subjects of international law. The natural person has increasingly become accepted as an independent actor subject to and benefiting from international law. Although natural persons are not parties to international law, they may bear rights and duties emanating from international law. Juridical persons—whether corporations or other business associations or registered non-governmental organizations, such as charities—similarly may bear rights and responsibilities under international law.

Finally, international organizations are subjects of international law that are comprised either solely or primarily of states. Examples of international organizations include the United Nations, the European Union, and the Organization of American States.

2. Individuals in the International Order

a. *Overview*

Historically, the subjects of international law have been states. International law may also apply to natural persons (individuals) and legal persons (such as corporations), all of which increasingly hold rights and obligations under international law. However, traditionally, such rights and obligations could only be enforced through states. Today, however, there are increasing treaties between states that enable individuals to bring suits before international tribunals and there are domestic laws that enable residents (both citizens and resident aliens) to sue states for torts or other wrongs suffered.

However, only states, and increasingly, international organizations, have full legal personality under international law; individuals only have legal personality in the international order to the extent that states allow. For example, individual victims of violations of international criminal law may refer the crime to a state prosecutor, who may bring the case before the International Criminal Court if the state has become a party thereto (art. 13(a) SICC).

In this chapter, we will explore the extent to which international law has enabled non-state actors (other than international organizations) to serve as subjects and objects in the international legal order.

b. *Examples of Individuals in the International Order*

Individuals may serve as subjects in the international order who may enforce their rights in national and international courts as well as objects in the international order who may be called to account for breaching their duties and responsibilities under international law. Among the examples of individuals in the international order, we may point to:

- Aliens as subjects of tort law against their states of residence (*e.g.*, ATCA)
- Individuals as objects who may be sued civilly under domestic law for the violation of international law (*e.g.*, ATCA);
- As subjects of international human rights law (*e.g.*, American Convention on Human Rights; European Convention on Human Rights; the ICCPR through its Human Rights Committee);
- As objects of international criminal law in venues such as the ICC or in *ad hoc* tribunals, such as the IMT (state actors) or the ICTY, ICTR, or SCSL (state and non-state actors).

D. Intersection of the Branches of International Law

Although the principles and customs of international law date back many centuries, the codification of international law is a relatively new phenomenon. Some of this codification, such as the Vienna Convention on the Law of Treaties, codifies principles that are already accepted in international customary law. Other developments in international law are innovative. For example, the Charter of the Nuremberg IMT laid down principles that were at the time novel, such as the principle that persons may be individually responsible for violations of international law.

The development and codification of international law is welcomed by many as bringing light to principles that otherwise have been uncertain. At the same time, because it is relatively new, there has been a great deal of overlap among the various branches of international law. For example, an crime may be classified as an international crime if it has an international dimension; if it is a crime that violates a basic right of an individual and is committed by a state, it may be classified as a human rights violation; if the same crime is committed in a systematic and organized fashion as part of a state policy, it may be considered a war crime in violation of international humanitarian law, as well as a human rights violation and an international crime. Thus, international institutions such as the ICC may be responsible for overseeing cases that fall not only into the category of international criminal law, but also human rights and international humanitarian and war law.

II. INTERNATIONAL ORGANIZATIONS AND INTERNATIONAL LAW

A. Overview

An international organization is a body created by a treaty with a permanent institutional structure whose membership consists either exclusively or in large part of states. The treaty is the constituent instrument of the organization. Although the main subject of international law has traditionally been the state, international law has evolved in the last century to include international and regional organizations. International organizations are subjects of international law because they have duties and rights under international law and can make international law.

One cannot understand international law without understanding the international organizations that make, apply, and enforce international law. Among these organizations, we can consider the United Nations, the European Union, NATO, and many others. Several of these organizations, such as the UN, OAS and EU, have their own legal arms that deal with issues ranging from international trade to human rights.

B. The United Nations

1. Overview of the United Nations

At the conclusion of World War I, the Treaty of Versailles, which established peace between Germany and the Allied Powers and established the League of Nations, was signed between Germany and the Allied Powers in 1919. However, because the Treaty required Germany to accept sole responsibility for causing the war and to make substantial territorial concessions and pay reparations deemed by many economists to be excessive, the Treaty was later largely ignored by Germany. The peace would ultimately collapse and the Treaty would be used by radical factions in Germany to win support for a nationalist cause that eventually gave rise to the Nazi Party and to World War II.

After the failure of the Treaty of Versailles and the League of Nations during World War II, the United Nations was founded in 1945 to maintain peace and security, develop friendly relations among nations, achieve international cooperation in solving international problems, and be a center for harmonizing the actions of the nations and attaining their common ends. The UN has been the locus for the development of binding laws and advisory standards, such as the Universal Declaration of Human Rights, and has established various organizations for the promulgation of rules ranging from labor to intellectual property standards. Among these organizations are the ILO, the World Health Organization, the World Intellectual Property Organization, the International Telecommunication Union, UNESCO, the World Trade Organization, and the International Monetary Fund.

2. Charter of the United Nations

a. Overview of the Charter

The Charter of the United Nations (CUN), together with the Statute of the International Court of Justice (SICJ), is the principal legal instrument of the UN. It was signed on 26 June 1945, in San Francisco, at the conclusion of the United Nations Conference on International Organization, and came into force on 24 October 1945. The CUN has been promulgated in order to achieve the UN's goals of attaining peace and security, friendly relations among nations, and international cooperation. The CUN has been adhered to by virtually all states; the few remaining non-member states have acquiesced in the principles established in the CUN.

b. *Preamble of the Charter*

The Charter consists of a Preamble and a series of articles grouped into chapters. The preamble consists of three parts:

- *An outline of the purposes for the establishment of the UN:* to save succeeding generations from the scourge of war; to affirm fundamental human rights and human dignity; to establish justice and respect for the rule of law; and to promote social progress and better standards of life;
- *A covenant among member states that agree to:* practice tolerance; unite strength to maintain peace and security; ensure that armed force not be used except in the common interest; and promote international economic and social progress; and
- A declaration that the governments of the peoples of the UN have agreed to the CUN.

c. *Body of the Charter*

The body of the Charter consists of nineteen chapters as follow:

- *Chapter I.* Sets forth the purposes and principles of the United Nations and provisions for the maintenance of international peace and security.
- *Chapter II.* Defines the criteria for membership in the United Nations, stating that the UN is "open to all other peace-loving states which accept the obligations contained in the present Charter and, in the judgment of the Organization, are able and willing to carry out these obligations" (art. 4.1 CUN).
- *Chapters III-V.* Describe the organs of the UN with specific attention given to the GA and SC.
- *Chapter VI.* Deals with the pacific settlement of disputes and the SC's power to investigate and mediate disputes (Ch. VI).
- *Chapters VII.* Outlines the SCs' power to take action in disputes through imposing sanctions and authorizing the use of military force in cases involving threats to and breaches of the peace and acts of aggression (Ch. VII). For further treatment, see "UN Collective Security Measures," *infra.*
- *Chapter VIII.* Makes possible regional arrangements for maintaining peace and security within their own regions;
- *Chapters IX and X.* Lay out a framework for international economic and social cooperation and establish ECOSOC, which oversees this framework.
- *Chapters XI-XIII.* A declaration regarding non-self-governing territories and an outline of the international trusteeship system, which oversaw decolonization.
- *Chapters XIV-XV.* Description of the ICJ and UN Secretariat and their respective powers and roles. *See supra.*, "Legal Institution: the International Court of Justice" for a full description of the ICJ and the SICJ.

- *Chapters XVI-XVII.* Miscellaneous provisions and transitional security arrangements related to World War II for integrating the UN with established international law.
- *Chapters XVIII-XIX.* The Charter amendment and ratification processes and signature by respective member governments.

3. Principal Non-Legal Organs

The UN is comprised of six principal organs: the General Assembly, the Security Council, ECOSOC, the Trusteeship Council, the Secretariat, and the International Court of Justice. In this section, we will examine the first five organs. In the following section, we will examine the International Court of Justice.

a. *The General Assembly (Ch. IV CUN)*

The General Assembly (GA), the main deliberative body of the UN, is composed of delegates of all member states. The decisions of the GA, which are made by a two-thirds majority or by a simple majority according to art. 18 CUN, largely mandate the activities and direction of the UN each year.

Apart from approval of budgetary matters regarding the allotment and collection of dues, the resolutions of the GA are not binding on UN members. The GA may make recommendations on any matters within the scope of the UN, except matters of peace and security under SC consideration. The GA may also adopt conventions, such as the 1948 Genocide Convention, that states are free to adopt and ratify. While the conventions on their own are not binding, they becomes binding on member states that sign and ratify them.

Although the resolutions of the GA are not legally binding *per se*, states sometimes express their opinions about the status of customary international law through declarations and recommendations of the GA, and this may in turn shape the content of customary international law. Furthermore, as will be mentioned below, the resolutions and declarations of international organizations such as the UN may constitute *opinio juris*, one of the five sources of international law.

b. *Security Council (Ch. V CUN)*

The SC has primary responsibility for the maintenance of international peace and security. It has the ability to make decisions that are legally binding on member states. Under the Charter, members of the UN agree to "accept and carry out the decisions of the Security Council in accordance with the present Charter" (art. 25 CUN). They thus agree that the decisions of the SC will be legally binding on them and on all other members. Under article 103 of the Charter, if there is a conflict "between the obligations of the Members of the United Nations under the present Charter and their obligations under any other international agreement, their obligations under the present Charter shall prevail." This means that if the SC adopts policies contrary to their other treaty obligations, states are required to abrogate their other treaty obligations.

c. *Economic and Social Council (Ch. X CUN)*

The Economic and Social Council (ECOSOC) coordinates the economic and social work of the United Nations and its specialized agencies and institutions. Voting in ECOSOC is by simple majority, with each member holding one vote.

d. Trusteeship Council (Ch. XII-XIII CUN).

The TC was established in 1945 to provide international supervision for eleven Trust Territories placed under the administration of seven Member States in order to adequately prepare them for self-governance. When these Trust Territories had attained self-government by 1994, the work of the TC had been completed.

e. Secretariat (Ch. XV CUN)

The Secretariat is the managerial body that carries out the day to day activities of the organization by servicing other organs and executing various tasks, such as peacekeeping administration and preparing studies.

4. Legal Institution: the International Court of Justice

a. Overview

The International Court of Justice (ICJ) was established by the Charter of the UN in June 1945 and began its work in 1946 as the "principal judicial organ of the United Nations" (art. 92 CUN). It is governed by the Statute of the International Court of Justice (SICJ), which is an integral part of the CUN. As the only one of the six principal UN organs not located in New York, the ICJ is seated in The Hague. The Court's stated objective is to settle in accordance with international law legal disputes submitted to it by states.

Although international law may regulate *some* of the relations between states and natural or juridical persons or international organizations and natural or juridical persons, the jurisdiction of the ICJ is limited to hearing only those cases in which all of the parties are states (art. 34.1 SICJ). Thus, non-state actors, including international organizations and individual and juridical persons, may not sue or be sued by states before the ICJ. Among the cases handled by the ICJ are the application and interpretation of international treaties and conventions, environmental issues, and border and law of the sea disputes between state actors. The ICJ may also hear international criminal and humanitarian law cases when all of the parties to a dispute are states, as was the case of the Bosnian genocide case (Bosnia and Herzegovina v. Serbia and Montenegro, case 91) that the court heard in 2006.

The ICJ is governed by chapter XIV of the CUN (arts. 92-96) as well as by the SICJ, is an integral part of the United Nations Charter that we examine below.

b. Provisions of the UN Charter with Respect to the ICJ

i. Peaceful Resolution of Disputes

The CUN establishes in its second article that "All Members ... shall fulfill in good faith the obligations assumed by them in accordance with the present Charter [and] settle their international disputes by peaceful means" (art. 2 CUN). Article 33 further requires parties to any dispute whose continuance is likely to endanger international peace and security to "seek a solution by negotiation, enquiry, mediation, conciliation, arbitration, judicial settlement, resort to regional agencies or arrangements, or other peaceful means of their own choice" (art 33 CUN). When such disputes arise, the SC may at any stage of a dispute "recommend appropriate procedures or methods of adjustment" (art. 36.1 CUN). In making such recommendations, the SC should "take into consideration that legal disputes should as a general rule be referred by the parties to the International Court of Justice in accordance with the provisions of the Statute of the Court" (art. 36.3 CUN).

ii. Open to All States

The ICJ is the court with the widest reach in the international landscape, as it is potentially open to all states. All members of the UN are *ipso facto* parties to the SICJ and agree to comply with the decision of the ICJ in any case to which they are parties. Furthermore, "a state which is not a Member of the United Nations may become a party to the Statute of the International Court of Justice on conditions to be determined in each case by the General Assembly upon the recommendation of the Security Council" (art. 93 CUN).

iii. Enforcement of Judgments

Each Member of the UN "undertakes to comply with the decision of the International Court of Justice in any case to which it is a party" (art. 94.1 CUN). Because UN members are obligated to obey decisions of the ICJ, the ICJ decisions have the power of binding law. If any party to a case fails to perform the obligations imposed by an ICJ judgment, the other party may have recourse to the SC, which may "make recommendations or decide upon measures to be taken to give effect to the judgment" (arts. 94.2 CUN).

iv. Types of Cases Handled by the ICJ

The ICJ principally handles the resolution of contentious disputes between states. In addition, the ICJ may give an advisory opinion on any legal question at the request of the GA or SC or on legal questions arising within the scope of the activities of other organs of the UN and specialized agencies, when their requests are authorized by the GA (art. 96 CUN, art. 65 SICJ).

c. *The Statute of the ICJ*

The SICJ establishes the ICJ as "the principal judicial organ of the United Nations" that is "constituted and shall function in accordance with the provisions of the present Statute" (art. 1 SICJ). The Statute is comprised of seventy articles divided into five chapters: Organization of the Court (arts. 2-33 SICJ); Competence of the Court (arts. 34-38 SICJ); Procedure (arts. 39-64 SICJ); Advisory Opinions (arts. 65-68); and Amendment (arts. 69-70 SICJ).

Under the Statute, the ICJ is to apply international conventions, international custom, the general principles of law "recognized by civilized nations," and "judicial decisions and the teachings of the most highly qualified publicists of the various nations, as subsidiary means for the determination of rules of law" (art. 38.1 SICJ). However, the application of these conventions and other legal sources "shall not prejudice the power of the Court to decide a case *ex aequo et bono* [by applying the rules of equity], if the parties agree thereto" (art. 38.2 SICJ). The may thus make a legal ruling based both on law as well as equity.

d. *ICJ Jurisdiction over Particular Cases*

Before the ICJ is able to adjudicate a particular contentious dispute among member states, its jurisdiction must be established. The CUN states that "All Members of the United Nations are *ipso facto* parties to the Statute of the International Court of Justice" (art. 93 CUN). However, neither the CUN nor the SICJ state that the ICJ holds jurisdiction over all disputes between member states. Rather, jurisdiction must be based on the consent of all of the parties under one of the following regimes:

i. Cases Referred to the ICJ on an Ad Hoc Basis (art. 36.1 SICJ)

The SICJ establishes jurisdiction of the ICJ over "all cases which the parties refer to it" (art. 36.1 SICJ). The ICJ thus has jurisdiction over those cases that states agree to bring before it. In this way, states may agree to the jurisdiction of the ICJ in specific matters, without conferring jurisdiction to the ICJ over all of their disputes.

ii. Compromissory Clause (art. 36.1 SICJ)

The SICJ further states that the jurisdiction of the Court comprises "all matters specially provided for in the Charter of the United Nations or in treaties and conventions in force" (art. 36.1 SICJ). This applies to states parties to a Convention, such as the Genocide Convention, that submits to the jurisdiction of the court any questions of interpretation or application.

iii. State Recognition of ICJ Compulsory Jurisdiction (art. 36.2 SICJ)

In addition, the SICJ declares in article 36.2 as follows:

> The states parties to the present Statute may at any time declare that they recognize as compulsory *ipso facto* and without special agreement, in relation to any other state accepting the same obligation, the jurisdiction of the Court in all legal disputes concerning: a. the interpretation of a treaty; b. any question of international law; c. the existence of any fact which, if established, would constitute a breach of an international obligation; d. the nature or extent of the reparation to be made for the breach of an international obligation.

Thus, if any two states have made this recognition, the ICJ will hold compulsory jurisdiction between them over any legal question arising under one of the four categories. States may withdraw their declaration to compulsory jurisdiction if they give reasonable notice (defined by the ICJ as six months in *Nicaragua v. United States of America* (ICJ)). Furthermore, their declarations "may be made unconditionally or on condition of reciprocity on the part of several or certain states, or for a certain time" (art. 36.3 SICJ). When a state makes such reservations, it is the ICJ that makes the final decision as to whether the Court has jurisdiction in the event that a dispute arises regarding the same (art. 36.6 SICJ).

iv. Carryover Jurisdiction from the Permanent Court of International Justice

Finally, if a state had granted jurisdiction to govern legal disputes to the Permanent Court of International Justice, this jurisdiction is carried over to the ICJ with respect to the same legal disputes.

C. The Council of Europe

1. Overview

The Council of Europe (COE) was founded in 1949 to work towards the integration of democratic development, freedom, the rule of law, and human rights throughout Europe. It currently has 47 member states comprising approximately 800 million citizens. Perhaps the most well known of the conventions of the COE is the 1950 Convention for the Protection of

Human Rights and Fundamental Freedoms (CPHR), colloquially known as the "European Convention on Human Rights."

2. Legal Institution: European Court of Human Rights

The COE has vested the European Court of Human Rights (ECHR), based in Strasbourg, France, with the power to hear cases involving the CPHR. Every state joining the COE must accede to the CPHR and agree to submit to the ECHR's compulsory jurisdiction for cases submitted by its individual nationals or foreign residents alleging human rights abuses in contravention to the CPHR.

The ECHR, as a supra-national court, provides legal recourse of last resort for individuals whose human rights have been violated by a contracting party to the CPHR. Before bringing suit to the ECHR, individuals must have exhausted the domestic legal proceedings that would have been capable of providing an adequate remedy for the breach of their Convention rights.

D. The European Union

1. Overview

The European Union (EU) was created after World War II to reduce trade barriers and increase cooperation among European nations. Through the European Commission, it has created significant bodies of legislation in a wide variety of areas including environmental law, commercial law, labor law, the law of the sea, air and space law, monetary law, and immigration law.

2. Legal Institution: the European Court of Justice

The European Court of Justice (ECJ), is the highest court in the European Union in matters of EU law. Established in 1952 and based in Luxembourg, the Court is tasked with interpreting EU law and ensuring its equal application across all EU member states. It is composed of one judge per member state and normally hears cases in panels of 3, 5, or 13 judges.

E. North Atlantic Treaty Organization

The North Atlantic Treaty Organization (NATO) is an international organization headquartered in Brussels and created in 1949 by the North Atlantic Treaty for the purpose of international collective security. As of 2010, NATO has 28 members: Albania, Belgium, Bulgaria, Canada, Croatia, Czech Republic, Denmark, Estonia, France, Germany, Greece, Hungary, Iceland, Italy, Latvia, Lithuania, Luxembourg, Netherlands, Norway, Poland, Portugal, Romania, Slovakia, Slovenia, Spain, Turkey, the United Kingdom, and the United States.

The North Atlantic Treaty sets out the resolve of the parties to "safeguard the freedom, common heritage and civilisation of their peoples, founded on the principles of democracy, individual liberty and the rule of law [and to] to promote stability and well-being in the North Atlantic area."

NATO was designed to be consistent in its purpose and functions with the obligations of UN member states contracted under the UN Charter. In the North Atlantic treaty, the parties recommit to "refrain in their international relations from the threat or use of force in any manner inconsistent with the purposes of the United Nations" (art. 1 NAT). However, the parties agree that "an armed attack against one or more of them in Europe or North America shall be considered an attack against them all" and that "if such an armed attack occurs, each of them, in exercise of the right of individual or collective self-defence recognised by Article 51 of the Charter of the United Nations, will assist the Party or Parties so attacked by taking forthwith, individually and in concert with the other Parties, such action as it deems necessary, including the use of armed force, to restore and maintain the security of the North Atlantic area" (art. 5 NAT).

F. The Organization of American States

1. Overview

The Organization of American States (OAS) is an international organization based in Washington, DC comprised of the 35 independent nations of the Americas. The Charter of the OAS (COAS) creating the organization was adopted by the nations of the Americas at the Ninth International Conference of American States in Bogotá, Colombia, in April 1948. Entering into force in 1951, the COAS sets out to achieve for its member nations "an order of peace and justice, to promote their solidarity, to strengthen their collaboration, and to defend their sovereignty, their territorial integrity, and their independence" (art. 1 COAS).

2. Legal Instruments

The American Declaration of the Rights and Duties of Man (ADRDM) was adopted by the nations of the Americas at the same meeting that created the OAS in 1948—the Ninth International Conference of American States in Bogotá. It was the world's first international human rights instrument and predated the UDHR by less than a year.

Although declarations in international law serve as sources of non-binding *opinio juris*, the jurisprudence of the Inter-American Court of Human Rights holds the ADRDM to be a source of binding international law for OAS member states. However, the ADRDM has been largely superseded by the more detailed American Convention on Human Rights (ACHR) (Pact of San José), adopted by the nations of the Americas meeting in San José, Costa Rica, in 1969, and entering into force in 1978.

At present, 24 of the 35 OAS member states have ratified the ACHR. The terms of the ADRDM apply to those nations that have not ratified the Convention, including Canada, the United States, and Cuba.

3. Legal Institutions

The bodies responsible for overseeing compliance with the ACHR are the Inter-American Commission on Human Rights (IACHR) and the Inter-American Court of Human Rights (IACtHR). The IACHR was created by the OAS in 1959 to promote the respect and defense of human rights in the Americas by investigating individual petitions alleging violations of the ADHR and resolving petitions in a collaborative way acceptable to both parties. Any person, group of persons or NGO may present a petition to the Commission alleging violations or failure to prevent violations by one of the OAS member states of the rights protected in the ADRDM or in the ACHR. The petitions presented to the Commission must show that the victim has exhausted domestic remedies.

The parties then exchange briefs and the Commission prepares a report including its conclusions and also generally its recommendations to the state concerned. The Commission gives the state a period of time to resolve the situation and to comply with its recommendations. Upon the expiration of this period of time, the Commission may either prepare a second report with recommendations that the state is to implement or it may take the case to the IACtHR.

The Inter-American Court of Human Rights was created by the OAS in 1979 to enforce and interpret provisions of the ACHR. It hears and makes decisions on human rights cases referred to it by IACHR and also may issue advisory opinions on matters of legal interpretation brought to it by OAS bodies or member states.

G. African Union

The AU was founded in 2002 in order to accelerate political and socio-economic integration in Africa; to promote and defend African common positions on issues of interest to the continent; to achieve peace and security on the continent, and to promote democratic institutions, good governance, and human rights. The AU is comprised of 53 members, Morocco being the only African state not in the Union.

The AU is the successor to the Organisation of African Unity (OAU), which was established in 1963 to promote the unity and solidarity of the African states and act as a collective voice for Africa and to eradicate all forms of colonialism.

III. SOURCES OF INTERNATIONAL LAW

A. Introduction

The Statute of the ICJ in its thirty eighth article indicates the following 4 sources of international law that apply to disputes submitted to it:

> a. international conventions, whether general or particular, establishing rules expressly recognized by the contesting states;
> b. international custom, as evidence of a general practice accepted as law;
> c. the general principles of law recognized by civilized nations;
> d. … judicial decisions and the teachings of the most highly qualified publicists of the various nations, as subsidiary means for the determination of rules of law" (art. 38 SICJ).

B. International Treaties and Conventions

The most important sources of international law are international treaties and conventions. These multilateral agreements govern the interaction of nations, multinational businesses, or nongovernmental organizations.

1. Overview

A treaty can be defined as a bilateral or multilateral agreement between states, between states and international organizations, or between international organizations that is governed by and binding under international law. According to the VCLT, treaties may be "embodied in a single instrument or in two or more related instruments" (art. 2(1)(a) VCLT). Treaties are generally in written form, and the VCLT includes the written form of treaties as part of their definition (art. 2(1)(a) VCLT), yet under customary international law, treaties do not necessarily need to be written.

Treaties are a source of international obligation for those states that agree to be bound by them. A unilateral law that governs the relations of a state with other states or that defines a state's foreign policies is not however a treaty if it is not binding on one or more other states or international organizations.

The designation of a treaty as such is not an essential element of the agreement. A treaty may thus be titled "agreement," "convention," or any other term that denotes the same, and yet still fall into the definition of a treaty.

2. Binding Force of Treaties

That treaties are binding on those states that agree to be bound by them is a general principle of law and is also established by international custom. States that agree to be bound by a treaty are known as "parties" to the treaty. States that sign a treaty are known as "signatories," and are not bound by a treaty until the state has agreed to be bound (usually through ratifying the treaty) and the treaty has entered into force.

To give further weight to the binding nature of treaties on parties to them, the VCLT establishes in its 26th article (*Pacta sunt servanda*) that "Every treaty in force is binding upon the parties to it and must be performed by them in good faith" (art. 26 VCLT). The VCLT is binding on the 111 state parties to the convention and other nations, such as the United States and France, which have not ratified the VCLT, are bound by their respective treaties under international custom and under the general principles of law, which consider the breach of a valid treaty to be a breach of international law. Thus, the breach of a provision of the VCLT by a state that has not ratified the VCLT would only be considered a breach of international law if the provision of the VCLT being breached were also a provision of international custom or of the general principles of law.

3.   Vienna Convention on the Law of Treaties

a.   *Consent to be Bound by Treaties*

The Vienna Convention on the Law of Treaties (VCLT) both codifies existing customary international law and adds to it. Signed at Vienna in 1969 and entering into force in 1980, it applies to treaties between states. Under the Convention, once a state consents to be bound to a treaty and a treaty enters into force, the state becomes a party bound by the treaty (art. 2(1)(g) VCLT). Consent to be bound by a treaty may be expressed "by signature, exchange of instruments constituting a treaty, ratification, acceptance, approval or accession, or by any other means if so agreed" (art. 11 VCLT).

The Convention goes on to explain the various ways that a state may express its intent to ratify, to be bound, and to accede to a treaty. In processes with both a signature and ratification, the signature demonstrates the intent to ratify, but not necessarily consent to be bound (art. 12 VCLT). Ratification is the act whereby a state expresses its consent to be bound (art. 14 VCLT) and in those cases where a state has not signed a treaty and the treaty is no longer open for signature, the state may "accede" to the treaty, whereby the state expresses its consent to be bound by the treaty (art. 15 VCLT).

In the period between a state's signing a treaty and the ratification of the treaty, or between the ratification of a treaty by a state and the entry into force of a treaty, the signatory or ratifying state may not undertake any actions that defeat the object and purpose of the treaty (art. 18 VCLT). However, this should not be construed to prohibit a state from unsigning a treaty that it no longer intends to ratify. If the state unsigns a treaty, it is no longer bound from taking actions that may defeat the object or purpose of the treaty.

b.   *Interpretation of Treaties*

"A treaty shall be interpreted in good faith in accordance with the ordinary meaning to be given to the terms of the treaty in their context and in the light of its object and purpose" (art. 31.1 VCLT). This context comprises:

-   any agreement relating to the treaty which was made between all the parties in connection with the conclusion of the treaty; and
-   any instrument which was made by one or more parties in connection with the conclusion of the treaty and accepted by the other parties as an instrument related to the treaty (art. 31.2 VCLT).

Recourse may be had to supplementary means of interpretation, including the preparatory work of the treaty (*travaux préparatoires*) and the circumstances of its conclusion, in order to confirm the meaning of the treaty (art. 32 VCLT).

c.   *Invalidity, Termination, and Suspension of Treaties*

Treaties may be held invalid for a variety of reasons, ranging from a state representative's incompetence to conclude a treaty to fraud, corruption, or duress or coercion (arts. 46-52 VCLT). Similarly, a treaty is void if at the time of its conclusion, it conflicts with peremptory norms of general international law (*jus cogens*) (art. 53 VCLT).

A treaty may be terminated or suspended as a consequence of its breach. A material breach of a bilateral treaty by one of the parties entitles the other to invoke the breach as a ground for terminating the treaty or suspending its operation (art. 60.1 VCLT).

The material breach of a multilateral treaty by one of the parties entitles the other parties by unanimous agreement to suspend the operation of the treaty or to terminate it in relation between themselves and the defaulting state or as between all the parties. A material breach of a multilateral treaty by one of the parties also entitles a party affected by the breach to invoke the breach as a ground for suspending the operation of the treaty in whole or in part in the relations between itself and the defaulting state and entitles any other party than the defaulting state to "invoke the breach as ground for suspending the operation of the treaty in whole or in part with respect to itself if the treaty is of such a character that the material breach of its provisions by one party radically changes the position of every party with respect to the further performance of its obligations under the treaty" (art. 60.2 VCLT).

A material breach may consist in: "(a) a repudiation of the treaty not sanctioned by the present Convention; or (b) the violation of a provision essential to the accomplishment of the object or purpose of the treaty" (art. 60.3 VCLT).

The decision of a state not to suspend or revoke a treaty that has been materially breached does not impair its ability to seek other means of compensation or reparation, including seeking damages or submitting to international arbitration.

C. Customary International Law

Customary international law can be defined according to the following three elements: (i) a consistent and recurrent state practice; (ii) developed over time; that is (iii) undertaken out of a sense of legal obligation. In this manner, the Restatement 3d of the Foreign Relations Law of the U.S. defines customary international law as resulting "from a general and consistent practice of states followed by them from a sense of legal obligation" (§ 102(2) RFR). This general and consistent practice is often referred to as "state practice." As the ICJ has declared in the Libya/Malta case (1985), this state practice, together with the *opinio juris* of states, forms the substance of customary law.

Although customary international law does not have to be universal, it must be widely enough practiced among states to qualify as "general" and "consistent" before it can serve as a source of the law. Widespread departure from customary international law may be an indication of the evolution of customary international law; if enough states adopt new practices, customary law may change and adopt the new practices as custom, even if these practices initially violate the customary international law in place at the time.

Historically, customary international law has been the most important source of international legal obligations and legal instruments such as the VCLT have been seen by some states as a mere restatement or codification of customary law.

We can determine the content of customary international law by looking to various sources, including the jurisprudential of international tribunals, the practices of international organs, and states' domestic laws and military and administrative practices.

If, during the development of a new rule of customary international law, a state repeatedly publicly announces its opposition to the rule, then the persistent objector will not be legally bound by the rule when it becomes customary law. This legal exemption will last as long as the state continues to object, unless the customary international law develops the status of *jus cogens* (a peremptory norm of general international law). If enough states object to the practice, then it will not become customary international law. If, however, a small group of states object to the practice, then they may develop their own special custom, which may be binding on them, but not on other nations, which would be bound by the customary law to which they implicitly or tacitly accepted.

D. General Principles of Law

Article 38 of the SICJ also defines "general principles of law recognized by civilized nations" as a source of international law. The general principles of law are used as gap fillers by international courts when there is no applicable treaty provision or rule of customary international law. The court will try to ascertain general principles of law by finding commonalities among well-development legal systems in the world. These general principles may include both principles of law and principles of equity.

Examples of general principles of law may be the notion that a contract to which assent was given through coercion or duress is null and void or that states are not permitted to interfere in the domestic affairs of other states.

E. *Opinio Juris:* Judicial Decisions and Teachings

Opinio juris is comprised of "the judicial decisions and the teachings of the most highly qualified publicists of the various nations" (art. 38 SICJ). *Opinio juris* may be comprised of not only judicial decisions and the writings of judges, scholars, and other experts, but also of the resolutions and declarations of international organizations.

Opinio juris is not itself a source of law, but it serves as a "subsidiary means for the determination of rules of law" (art. 38 SICJ). Furthermore, *opinio juris* in a case before the ICJ is only binding "between the parties and in respect of that particular case" (art. 59 SICJ). While the analyses of judicial decisions and experts may be helpful in determining what the law is, they are binding only with respect to the parties and issues of a particular case.

F. International Declarations

States may make declarations, such as the UDHR, which are not legally binding. Such declarations are considered to be "soft law": although they are not legally binding, they may influence states by placing political, rather than legal, pressure on their actions. Such declarations may also be effective when states are uncertain as to whether other states are ready to undertake the commitment of submitting to binding laws and they may serve as intermediate steps towards the formation of future treaties or other legal instruments.

International declarations, if ratified by enough states and practiced by them out of a sense of legal obligation, can become sources of binding customary international law.

IV. STATES AND GOVERNMENTS IN THE INTERNATIONAL ORDER

A. Overview

We begin by highlighting an important distinction between "states" and "governments." States are bearers of rights and responsibilities under international law; governments represent them. As a general rule, a change in government does not affect the international obligations of the state.

In the past 50 years, there has been a rapid increase in the number of states that exist. This is evidenced by the vast increase in members of the UN. When the UN was formed in 1945, it had only 51 member states; today, it has 191. This increase can be attributed to a variety of causes, among which we may list decolonization and the break up of states such as the USSR, Yugoslavia, Czechoslovakia, and Ethiopia (with Eritrea breaking away).

Break-ups of states occur through dissolution or secession. In the case of dissolution, an existing state implodes and becomes two or more new states (*e.g.*, Yugoslavia and Czechoslovakia). In secession, part of an existing state breaks away to become a new state (*e.g.*, the break away of Eritrea from Ethiopia), with the new state holding the right to govern its own citizens, to enter into treaties, join international organizations, or be a state party to an ICJ case.

B. Criteria for Statehood

Although the distinction has narrowed recently, there are two traditional theories that provide guidance as to the legal recognition of an entity's sovereignty in the international community: (i) the declarative theory; and (ii) the constitutive theory.

1. Objective Test under the Declarative Theory

The declarative theory is the prevailing theory for the recognition of state sovereignty. It holds that an entity is recognized as a state when it satisfies the following objective criteria for statehood, which were laid down in the Montevideo Convention of 1933:

- *Permanent Population*. The size is incidental, but what is important is that the population not consist of seasonal inhabitants or people simply passing through.
- *Defined Territory*. The size of the territory is incidental, but the state must consider itself to have exclusive authority over some defined territory. The borders of this territory may be disputed, yet the government must hold to a fixed position.
- *Effective Government*. There must be a government with effective control over the territory, though there are times where states are recognized even though there is a civil war and no single entity that is in effective control of the whole territory (*e.g.*, Somalia). This is due to states' reluctance to revoke their longstanding recognition of other states that have long been established by the international community, as doing so would create international legal instability.
- *Capacity to Enter Relations with Other States*. The state must be able to enter into relations with other states. Examples of such relations include the establishment of diplomatic missions and the conclusion of bilateral treaties.

Under the declarative theory, an entity is deemed a state based on these four criteria, regardless of its recognition as one by other states.

2. State Recognition under the Constitutive Theory

Under the constitutive theory, an entity is not a state unless it is recognized as such by the international community. "Recognition" refers to the formal acknowledgement by other states that an entity is a state. This recognition implies a political decision, one that each country takes of its own accord and volition. In this way, the constitutive theory is based on a legal construct and is usually invoked by entities when a majority of the international community recognizes them as states.

Recognition has important consequences. It grants effective title to territory as well title to assets or other property that may be held abroad. It also bolsters the claim to statehood based on the declaratory theory.

Individual states may condition recognition of new states on certain criteria, above and beyond those that comprise the declarative theory. For example, the European Community, which preceded the EU, declared conditioned its recognition of new states of the Eastern bloc on their commitments to human rights and nuclear non-proliferation.

3. Number of Recognized Sovereign States

There are 193 sovereign states recognized by the international community: the 192 UN member states and Vatican City. While Vatican City is an independent state with its own population, territory, government, and ability to enter into relations with other states, it has chosen not to join the global body.

In addition to these 193 states, there are a handful of territories whose sovereignty is disputed. Kosovo is one such example. While there are at the time of writing 71 states that recognize Kosovo's sovereignty, there are approximately 100 that have implicitly or explicitly denied Kosovo's independence. Thus, although the ICJ has ruled that Kosovo's declaration of independence does not violate international law, the status of Kosovo as an independent state under the constitutive theory is as of yet uncertain.

Taiwan stands in a similar position. While it has its own population, defined territory, effective government, and ability to enter into relations with other countries (Taiwan has established in several countries bureaus for cultural and economic affairs similar to embassies), its status as an independent country has largely been disputed, and China uses its Security Council membership, which was transferred to the PRC from the RC in 1971, on the to assure that no resolutions recognizing Taiwan as an independent state are permitted to move forward. Thus, although Taiwan fulfills the criteria for statehood, it is not to be considered a sovereign, independent state under the constitutive theory, because the international community has not recognized it as a state.

C. Recognition of Governments

The following are three doctrines that may help inform whether a government will be recognized by other states:

1. Traditional Approach

States consider four factors in deciding whether to recognize a state: (i) the effectiveness of control; (ii) stability and permanence; (iii) ability and willingness to fulfill obligations; and (iv) popular support. Popular support does not necessarily means that the government must be democratic; it simply means that the people acquiescence to the government. This is to assure that the government is internally stable before being recognized by other states.

2. Estrada Doctrine

When a new government comes to power through constitutional means or otherwise, its relations with other states remain unchanged. Although Mexico no longer follows this doctrine, it was created by the Mexican government, which found that it would be insulting to make determinations about recognition of governments because it would involve passing judgment on the internal affairs of other states.

3. Tobar Doctrine

Under this doctrine, states will not recognize governments which come into power as a consequence of a coup or of a revolution against the government, so long as the freely elected representatives of the people thereof have not constitutionally reorganized the country. Over the past decade, the US and other countries have spent a great deal of resources writing about the importance of democratic governance as a new trend, and the OAS has adopted significant resolutions in this spirit. In some cases, the UN will not allow a government to take a seat at the UN when the government was not democratically installed.

D. Jurisdiction

Questions of jurisdiction in civil matters are generally resolved by applying conflict of laws rules. The issue becomes important in international law when the assertion of jurisdiction by a state affects foreign nationals.

It is a general principle of law that states may exercise jurisdiction over nationals with whom they have sufficient contacts. It may be a general principle of law that states may exercise jurisdiction over subject matters when the ties to a subject matter are sufficiently close to override the interests of a competing state.

1. Territorial Principle

The primary basis for jurisdiction is a state's territory: states may legislate and apply legislation within their territories, unless treaties provide otherwise. This principle allows states to apply their legislation to any individual located within their territory, whether they are nationals or aliens.

the courts of a state may adjudicate any legal or factual issues when the case or controversy arise in the state's own territory.

2. Nationality Principle

A second basis for jurisdiction is nationality: a state may regulate the activities of both its nationals located in the home state as well as its nationals located abroad. Most states have laws that require that their nationals who commit crimes abroad be tried at home, and to this end extradition treaties have been established.

E. Legality of the Use of Force

1. Introduction

Both customary international law as well as the UN Charter recognize the territorial integrity and independence of states and prohibit military force from interfering with this integrity and independence. The CUN states that "All Members shall settle their international disputes by peaceful means in such a manner that international peace and security, and justice, are not endangered" and that "All Members shall refrain in their international relations from the threat or use of force against the territorial integrity or political independence of any state, or in any other manner inconsistent with the Purposes of the United Nations" (art. 2 CUN).

Chapter VII of the UN Charter permits two exceptions to these blanket prohibitions; the use of force is permitted when acting pursuant to: (i) UN collective security measures (arts. 42 CUN); or (ii) self-defense (art. 51 CUN).

2. Use of Force as a Collective Security Measure (art. 42 CUN)

The first exception is the right of the SC to employ the use of force in order to secure peace. If the SC determines the existence of any threat to or breach of the peace or act of aggression, it is to make recommendations or decide what measures are to be taken to maintain or restore peace (art. 39 CUN). In order to prevent an aggravation of the situation, the SC may "call upon the parties concerned to comply with such provisional measures as it deems necessary or desirable" (art. 40 CUN), and may decide what measures not involving the use of armed force (*e.g.*, sanctions, the severance of diplomatic relations) are to be employed to give effect to its decisions (art. 41 CUN). However, if these measures are inadequate or ineffective, the SC may take military action "by air, sea, or land forces as may be necessary to maintain or restore international peace and security" (art. 42 CUN), as it did in the Persian Gulf War (1990-91). To this end, all UN members are to make available to the SC "armed forces, assistance, and facilities, including rights of passage" (art. 43 CUN).

The Security Council shall, when appropriate, utilize regional arrangements or agencies "for enforcement action under its authority. But no enforcement action shall be taken under regional arrangements or by regional agencies without the authorization of the Security Council, with the exception of measures against any enemy state," which is in turn defined as "a state that during the Second World War had been an enemy of any signatory" of the CUN (art. 53 CUN). Thus, even a regional organization such as NATO must act with authorization from the SC prior to undertaking a military act.

3. Use of Force in Self-Defense (art. 51 CUN)

The second exception is the use of force pursuant to states' inherent right to self-defense; states may use force as a last resort when threatened by armed attacks. This principle is also embedded in customary international law. However, the CUN only permits this right to be exercised "*until* the Security Council has taken measures necessary to maintain international peace and security" (art. 51 CUN). A state may thus only act out of self-defense until the SC actually takes *action*. Article 51 further requires measures taken by members in the exercise of this right to be "immediately reported to the Security Council" (art. 51 CUN).

F. Territory

One of the fundamental elements of a sovereign state is a defined territory subject to the exclusive jurisdiction and governance of the state. The territory of a state may be expanded through:

- *Cession*. Other states may cede territory to a state (*see Island of Palmas Case* between the US and the Netherlands at the Permanent Court of Arbitration (1928));
- *Terra nullius*. States may obtain title to land not under the sovereignty or control of any state—*terra nullius* (*Lat.*, "the land of no one")—through the occupation thereof.
- *Prescription*. A state acquires title to a territory by practicing uncontested sovereignty thereon over an uninterrupted period of time.

Under modern international law, military conquest is not a valid means of territorial expansion. Title to territory cannot be acquired through the use of force alone; express or implied consent is a prerequisite before international recognition of the new title will be conferred.

The ICJ, acting under its contentious jurisdiction, may hear and resolve territorial disputes cases, as it did in *Botswana v. Namibia* (1999), ruling in favor of Botswana's claim over Sedudu Island.

V. INTERNATIONAL HUMANITARIAN LAW: THE LAW OF ARMED CONFLICT

A. Introduction

1. Overview

International humanitarian law (IHL), also known as the law of war, the law of armed conflict, or *jus in bello*, is an area of international law that concerns the protection of members of armed forces and civilians during wars, armed conflicts, and military occupations of territories. IHL sets standards for the humanitarian treatment of victims and prisoners of war, seeks to limit the effects of armed conflict on civilians who are not or are no longer participating in hostilities, and restricts the means and methods of warfare.

2. Origins

The law of war can be said to have originated with the Dutch jurist Hugo Grotius (1583-1645), whose writings established the basis of international law based on natural law. In his treatise *De jure belli ac pacis libri tres* (*On the Law of War and Peace: Three books*), published in 1625, Grotius advances a system of principles of natural law, whereby what is "just" is consistent with the nature of a society of rational beings. He holds these principles to be binding on all people and nations regardless of local custom, and then goes on to outline the circumstances under which war may be justly executed. The book is divided into three parts, as follow:

- *Book I: General conception.* Offers a conception of war and of natural justice, arguing that there are some circumstances in which war is justifiable.
- *Book II: Jus ad bellum (justice in the resort to war).* Describes three "just causes" for war: self-defense, reparation of injury, and punishment; Grotius considers a wide variety of circumstances under which these causes apply.
- *Book III: Jus in bello (justice in the conduct of war).* Enumerates the rules governing the conduct of war once it has begun. Grotius argues that all parties to war are bound by such rules, whether or not their cause is just.

The purposes of the law of armed conflict are fourfold:

- Limit the damages, casualties, and other consequences of conflict;
- Protect combatants and civilians from unnecessary suffering;
- Guarantee the fundamental rights of combatants and civilians; and
- Prevent the escalation of conflict.

3. International Humanitarian Law and Human Rights Law

In some ways, IHL can be viewed as a set of specialized human rights regulations that apply during war and armed conflict. However, this does not mean that ordinary human rights regulations cease to be operational when IHL is applied. Rather, it means that, unless normal human rights law is derogated by treaty or otherwise, the rules of IHL apply in addition to human rights law.

For example, in a state where domestic law prohibits discrimination by state actors (a domestic human rights provision, often termed a "civil right" because it is domestic), citizens of that state that continue to enjoy the right to be free from discrimination even if their territory were being occupied by a foreign military force. During such an occupation, not only would IHL's regulations providing for the protection of civilians and civilian objects, the care for the sick and the wounded, the treatment of POWs, and limitations on the use of weapons and methods of war apply, but those provisions of domestic or international human rights law, such as the right to be free from discrimination, would continue to apply, whether civilians in the occupied territory were under the authority of their own civil government or of the foreign occupation force.

B. Principles of International Humanitarian Law

1. Protection of Persons

a. *Distinction (Discrimination)*

Parties to a conflict must at all times distinguish between the civilian population and combatants in order to spare civilian population and property.

- *Civilians*. An attacker may not intentionally attack civilians or employ methods that would cause excessive collateral casualties among protected civilians. Civilians may, however, lose their protected status if the defender fails to separate civilians and civilian objects from military targets.
- *Civilian Objects*. This principle imposes a requirement to distinguish, or discriminate, between military objects, which may be targets of an attack, and civilian objects, which may not be targeted. Civilian objects such as places of worship, hospitals, and dwellings may, however, lose their protected status if they become tools for military action.

b. *Proportionality with Respect to Civilian Losses*

Those who plan military operations must take into consideration the extent of civilian destruction and probable casualties that will result and, to the extent consistent with the necessities of the military situation, seek to avoid or minimize such casualties and destruction. While civilian losses must be proportionate to the military advantages sought, this principle must be consistent with the allowable risk to the attacking force; the attacker need not expose himself to excessive risk simply in order to minimize civilian losses.

2. Conduct, Weapons, Use of Force

a. *Military Necessity*

Military necessity permits the application of only that degree of regulated force required for the partial or complete submission of the enemy with the least expenditure of life, time and resources. Attacks must be limited to military objects, which by their nature, location, purpose, or use make an effective contribution to military action and whose total or partial destruction, capture, or neutralization offers a definite military advantage (*e.g.*, troops, supplies, headquarters).

Parties to a conflict and members of their armed forces do not have an unlimited choice of methods and means of warfare. It is prohibited to employ weapons or methods of warfare of a nature to cause unnecessary losses or excessive suffering.

b. Humanity

The right of parties to a conflict to adopt means of injuring the enemy is not unlimited. Also known as the principle of unnecessary suffering, the principle of humanity prohibits the employment of any degree of force that is not necessary for the purposes of military mission accomplishment by causing unnecessary losses or excessive suffering.

C. Protection of Persons in Armed Conflicts: the Geneva Conventions

1. Overview

The Geneva Conventions comprise four treaties and three additional protocols. Prior to the first Geneva Convention of 1864, only customary law applied to the conduct of states at war. It was only with the first Geneva Convention that the rules of armed conflict were codified. Prior to the Convention, the nations' customs and traditions governing the conduct of war varied among states or were temporary.

After the Geneva Conventions were adopted, clear sets of rules were defined to require those engaged in armed conflict to respect IHL and to ensure the respect of IHL. While the ICRC is regarded as the "guardian" of the Geneva Conventions and other treaties that constitute IHL, it cannot serve as policeman or judge. These functions belong to states parties to international treaties, who are required to respect IHL, ensure the respect of IHL, and punish those responsible for "grave breaches" of the Geneva Conventions.

2. Main Principles

3. Conventions Preceding the 1949 Geneva Conventions

The governments of Europe and America came together in 1864 to establish rules governing conduct during warfare. The resulting Convention of 1864 was replaced by the Geneva Conventions of 1906, 1929 and 1949, all of which expanded the original and added provisions relating to war at sea, prisoners of war, and civilians. The original treaties continued to have binding force only between those countries that did not ratify the later treaties.

a. Geneva Convention of 1864 for the Wounded in War

After the termination of the Geneva Conference of 1863, the Swiss Federal Council invited the governments of Europe and America to a diplomatic conference to adopt a convention for the amelioration of the condition of the wounded in war. The conference adopted a treaty comprised of ten articles—the Convention for the Amelioration of the Condition of the Wounded in Armies in the Field (Geneva, 1864), which provides relief to the sick and the wounded without distinction as to nationality. The wounded and sick must be collected and cared for by the party that has them in its power, and this protection was extended to medical personnel, establishments, transports and equipment. The Convention established the neutrality of medical personnel and medical establishments and units, and the distinctive signs of the red cross, red crescent or the red lion and sun on a white ground were established as signs of such protection.

The 1864 Convention ceased to have effect in 1966 when the Republic of Korea, the last party to the 1864 Convention that had not acceded to a later Convention, acceded to the 1949 Conventions.

b. Geneva Convention of 1906 for the Wounded and Shipwrecked at Sea

Several proposals were made after 1864 to revise the 1864 Convention of 1864. A conference was convened at Geneva in 1868 to adapt the principles of the 1864 Convention to sea warfare, but the additional articles were not ratified. The 1899 Hague Peace Conference proposed a special conference for the revision of the Geneva Convention of 1864, and this resulted in a 1906 Conference attended by 35 states that adopted the Convention for the Amelioration of the Condition of the Wounded and Sick in Armies in the Field. This new Convention replaced the old as between the contracting states.

With 33 articles rather than 10, the 1906 Convention is more detailed than the former and adds additional provisions for wounded, sick, and shipwrecked soldiers at sea during war, while changing some provisions. For example, the duty to repatriate the wounded who are unfit for further service was transformed into a recommendation.

c. Geneva Convention of 1929 for Prisoners of War

Provisions relating to the treatment of prisoners of war are contained in the 1899 and 1907 Hague Regulations. Due to their imprecision, the ICRC drafted a convention that would complete the Hague regulations by including a prohibition of reprisals and collective penalties, the organization of prisoners' work, and prisoners' designation of representatives. The Diplomatic Conference of Geneva adopted the Convention relative to the Treatment of Prisoners of War on July 27, 1929, containing 97 articles and an Annex model draft agreement concerning the direct repatriation or accommodation in a neutral country of prisoners of war for reasons of health.

4. Geneva Conventions of 1949

The pre-1949 Geneva Conventions are all concerned primarily with combatants rather than with civilians. The events of World War II showed the disastrous consequences of the absence of a treaty protecting civilians in wartime. Thus, in 1949, the preceding three Conventions were revised and a fourth Convention was adopted to provide for the protection of civilians from the consequences of war. The results were the four 1949 Geneva Conventions, dealing with the treatment and protections of persons—both combatant and civilian—during armed conflict.

The 1949 Geneva Conventions have been ratified, in whole or with reservations, by 194 countries, thus making the Conventions universally applicable. They deal with the following issues:

- Protections for the wounded and for civilians in and around a war zone;
- The rights of those captured during a military conflict and rules for the treatment of civilian internees;

- The status and treatment of protected persons, including civilian populations in occupied territory, and provisions on humanitarian relief for these populations.

a. Geneva Convention (I) for the Wounded in the Field

Containing 64 articles, the Geneva Convention (I) for the Amelioration of the Condition of the Wounded and Sick in Armed Forces in the Field sought to protect wounded and sick soldiers on land during war. Soldiers who have laid down their arms or who are otherwise *hors de combat* are entitled to respect for their lives and their moral and physical integrity. It is forbidden to kill or injure them. This protection also extends to medical and religious personnel, medical units, and medical transports.

Convention (I) also contains two annexes containing a draft agreement relating to hospital zones and a model identity card for medical and religious personnel.

b. Geneva Convention (II) for the Wounded, Sick and Shipwrecked at Sea

The Geneva Convention (II) for the Amelioration of the Condition of Wounded, Sick and Shipwrecked Members of Armed Forces at Sea protects wounded, sick and shipwrecked military personnel at sea during war. It replaced the Hague Convention of 1907 for the Adaptation to Maritime Warfare of the Principles of the Geneva Convention. Its content closely follows the first Geneva Convention, but its 63 articles specifically apply to war at sea by protecting, for example, hospital ships. It has one annex containing a model identity card for medical and religious personnel.

c. Geneva Convention (III) for the Treatment of Prisoners of War

The Geneva Convention (III) relative to the Treatment of Prisoners of War. Geneva replaced the Prisoners of War Convention of 1929. With 143 articles, it is more detailed than the 1929 Convention. It defines the categories of persons entitled to prisoner of war status and the rights outlined in the Convention. These rights belong not only to members of the armed forces or of militias, but also to members of volunteer corps forming part of such armed forces as well as to persons who "accompany the armed forces without actually being members thereof, such as civilian members of military aircraft crews, war correspondents, supply contractors, members of labour units or of services responsible for the welfare of the armed forces" (art. 4 GC III).

Convention (III) also defines the conditions and places of captivity, particularly with regard to the labor of prisoners of war, their financial resources and payment of a fair working rate, their right to send and receive letters and cards, and the relief they receive. The Convention established the principle of repatriating prisoners of war immediately upon the cessation of hostilities.

The judicial proceedings instituted against POWs are dealt with in part III of Chapter III. This section prohibits trying or sentencing any POW under any *ex post facto* law (art. 99 GC III). Unlike common article 3, which applies only to non-international conflicts and prohibits "the passing of sentences and the carrying out of executions without previous judgment pronounced by a regularly constituted court affording all the judicial guarantees" (art. 3(1)(d) GC III), article 102 implies that such guarantees are not required if they are not the detaining state's custom with regard to members of its own armed forces: "A prisoner of war can be validly sentenced only if the sentence has been pronounced by the same courts according to the same procedure as in the case of members of the armed forces of the Detaining Power" (art. 102 GC III). Thus, in countries such as the United States, where members of the armed forces may be tried by special courts marshal (military courts), POWs are not entitled to civilian trials and all of their guarantees. At the same time, GC III requires that the POW have access to a "defence by a qualified advocate or counsel of his own choice, to the calling of witnesses and ... to the services of a competent interpreter" (art. 105 GC III).

The five annexes of Convention (III) contain various model regulations and model identity and other cards.

d. Geneva Convention (IV) for the Protection of Civilian Persons in Time of War

Perhaps the most fundamental norm of international humanitarian law today is contained in the Geneva Convention (IV) relative to the Protection of Civilian Persons in Time of War: states may not directly target civilians in military attacks. Taking into account the experience of WWII, where civilians were systematically targeted in both internal as well as international conflicts, the fourth Convention contains provisions regarding the general protection of populations against the consequences of war and promulgates regulations governing the status and treatment of protected persons. The Fourth Convention is supplementary to the provisions of the Hague Regulations of 1907 (art. 154 GC IV). The three annexes of the Fourth Convention contain a model agreement on hospital and safety zones, model regulations on humanitarian relief, and model cards.

5. Application of the 1949 Geneva Conventions: Common Articles 2 and 3

a. Common Article 2: International Conflicts

Under common article 2 of the Geneva Conventions (common to the four Geneva Conventions), the Conventions apply to "all cases of declared war or of any other armed conflict which may arise between two or more of the High Contracting Parties, even if the state of war is not recognized by one of them [as well as to] all cases of partial or total occupation of the territory of a High Contracting Party." Furthermore, in a conflict between three or more powers, "although one of the Powers in conflict may not be a party to the present Convention, the Powers who are parties thereto shall remain bound by it in their mutual relations." If a non-party to the Convention accepts and applies the provisions of the Conventions, the states parties "shall furthermore be bound by the Convention" in relation to the said non-party (common article 2 Geneva Conventions).

b. Common Article 3: Internal Conflicts

The Geneva Conventions also codify the rules of engagement in non-international (domestic) armed conflict. Common article 3 of the Geneva Conventions is the first express codification of laws for non-international armed conflicts, such as civil wars, civil insurrections, internal armed conflicts that spill over into other states or internal conflicts in which third states or a multinational force intervenes alongside the government. Common article 3 establishes fundamental rules from which no derogation is permitted and whose violation gives rise to individual rather than state liability. It is like a mini-Convention within the Conventions as it contains the essential rules of the Geneva Conventions as applied to conflicts of a domestic character. It applies to all non-combatants, including soldiers who have "laid down their arms" (surrendered) or those placed *hors de combat* due to injury or sickness and protects them from the following:

- Violence, murder, inhumane treatment, and torture;
- Taking of hostages;
- Outrages upon personal dignity, including degrading treatment; and
- The passing of sentences and the carrying out of executions through unfair trials or without "previous judgment pronounced by a regularly constituted court affording all the judicial guarantees which are recognized as indispensable by civilized peoples" (art. 3(1) GC III). This provision *only applies in the case of internal conflict*. In the case of international conflicts, states may judge prisoners by special military courts (see part III of Chapter III of Geneva Convention (III)).

Common article 3 further requires that the wounded, sick and shipwrecked be collected and cared for and grants the ICRC and other impartial humanitarian bodies the right to offer their services to the parties to the conflict. It calls on the parties to the conflict to endeavor to bring all or parts of the Geneva Conventions into force through special agreements and recognizes that the application of these rules does not affect the legal status of the parties to the conflict (art. 3(2) GC III).

6. Grave Breaches

States parties to the Convention are required to respect IHL, ensure the respect of IHL, and seek out and try persons alleged to have committed "grave breaches" of the Geneva Conventions (art. 146 GC IV) and to punish those responsible for such breaches. If breaches of the Geneva Conventions are perpetrated against protected persons, all states have an obligation to find the perpetrators and bring them to justice. The Fourth Convention defines grave breaches as "any of the following acts, if committed against persons or property protected by the present Convention: wilful killing, torture or inhuman treatment, including biological experiments, wilfully causing great suffering or serious injury to body or health, unlawful deportation or transfer or unlawful confinement of a protected person, compelling a protected person to serve in the forces of a hostile Power, or wilfully depriving a protected person of the rights of fair and regular trial prescribed in the present Convention, taking of hostages and extensive destruction and appropriation of property, not justified by military necessity and carried out unlawfully and wantonly" (art. 147 GC IV). In *Prosecutor v. Dusko Tadic* (1999), the ICTY held that grave breaches apply not only to international conflicts, but also to internal armed conflicts as well. Further, those provisions are considered customary international law, allowing war crimes prosecution even over groups that have not formally accepted the terms of the Geneva Conventions.

D. Weapons and Methods of War: Hague Conventions and other Treaties

1. Hague Conventions (1899 and 1907)

The Hague Conventions are a group of international treaties aimed at regulating the conduct of war and limiting certain types of military technology. The Conventions were adopted in the 1899 and 1907 Hague conferences.

a. Hague Conventions of 1899

The Conventions adopted on July 29, 1899, at the 1899 Hague Conference are as follow:

- Final Act of the International Peace Conference (state signatories - 27);
- Convention (I) for the Pacific Settlement of International Disputes (creating the Permanent Court of Arbitration "with the object of facilitating an immediate recourse to arbitration for international differences" (art. 20));
- Convention (II) with Respect to the Laws and Customs of War on Land and its annex: Regulations concerning the Laws and Customs of War on Land (state parties - 49);
- Convention (III) for the Adaptation to Maritime Warfare of the Principles of the Geneva Convention of 22 August 1864 (state parties - 49);
- Declaration (IV,1), to Prohibit, for the Term of Five Years, the Launching of Projectiles and Explosives from Balloons, and Other Methods of Similar Nature (state parties - 24; state signatories - 2);
- Declaration (IV,2) concerning Asphyxiating Gases (state parties - 31);
- Declaration (IV,3) concerning Expanding Bullets (state parties - 31).

b. *Hague Conventions of 1904 and 1906*

The 1904 and 1906 Conventions are as follow:

- Convention for the Exemption of Hospital Ships, in Time of War, from The Payment of all Dues and Taxes Imposed for the Benefit of the State. 21 December 1904 (state parties - 31; state signatories - 1);
- Convention for the Amelioration of the Condition of the Wounded and Sick in Armies in the Field. Geneva, 6 July 1906 (state parties - 52; state signatories - 5).

c. *Hague Conventions of 1907*

i. Overview

The Conventions adopted on October 18, 1907, at the 1907 Hague Conference are as follow (those with continuing validly are in bold italics):

- Final Act of the Second Peace Conference (state signatories - 44);
- Convention (I) for the Pacific Settlement of International Disputes;
- Convention (II) for the Limitation of Employment of Force for Recovery of Contract Debts;
- ***Convention (III) relative to the Opening of Hostilities*** (state parties - 34; state signatories - 17);
- ***Convention (IV) respecting the Laws and Customs of War on Land and its annex: Regulations concerning the Laws and Customs of War on Land*** (state parties - 35; state signatories - 15);
- ***Convention (V) respecting the Rights and Duties of Neutral Powers and Persons in Case of War on Land*** (state parties - 32; state signatories - 17);
- Convention (VI) relating to the Status of Enemy Merchant Ships at the Outbreak of Hostilities (state parties - 29; state signatories - 19);
- Convention (VII) relating to the Conversion of Merchant Ships into War-Ships (state parties - 32; state signatories - 16);

- *Convention (VIII) relative to the Laying of Automatic Submarine Contact Mines* (state parties - 27; state signatories - 17);
- *Convention (IX) concerning Bombardment by Naval Forces in Time of War* (state parties - 35; state signatories - 16);
- Convention (X) for the Adaptation to Maritime Warfare of the Principles of the Geneva Convention (state parties - 33; state signatories - 16);
- Convention (XI) relative to certain Restrictions with regard to the Exercise of the Right of Capture in Naval War (state parties - 31; state signatories - 17);
- Convention (XII) relative to the Creation of an International Prize Court (state parties - 1; state signatories - 31);
- Convention (XIII) concerning the Rights and Duties of Neutral Powers in Naval War (state parties - 28; state signatories - 18);
- Declaration (XIV) Prohibiting the Discharge of Projectiles and Explosives from Balloons (state parties - 20; state signatories - 12).

ii. Hague Convention IV of 1907

Perhaps the most important of the Hague Conventions is Convention (IV) respecting the Laws and Customs of War on Land and its Annex (HC IV). The Annex is comprised of Regulations concerning the Laws and Customs of War on Land. These regulations establish the principle of humanity (also known as the principle of unnecessary suffering), which prohibits the employment of any degree of force that is not necessary for the purposes of military mission accomplishment and causes unnecessary losses or excessive suffering. Article 22 sets out this principle when it states that "the right of belligerents to adopt means of injuring the enemy is not unlimited" (art. 22 HC IV) and article 23 follows up by making the following acts specifically forbidden:

- "(a)   To employ poison or poisoned weapons;
- (b)   To kill or wound treacherously individuals belonging to the hostile nation or army;
- (c)   To kill or wound an enemy who, having laid down his arms, or having no longer means of defence, has surrendered at discretion;
- (d)   To declare that no quarter will be given;
- (e)   To employ arms, projectiles, or material calculated to cause unnecessary suffering;
- (f)   To make improper use of a flag of truce, of the national flag or of the military insignia and uniform of the enemy, as well as the distinctive badges of the Geneva Convention;
- (g)   To destroy or seize the enemy's property, unless such destruction or seizure be imperatively demanded by the necessities of war;
- (h)   To declare abolished, suspended, or inadmissible in a court of law the rights and actions of the nationals of the hostile party. A belligerent is likewise forbidden to compel the nationals of the hostile party to take part in the operations of war directed against their own country, even if they were in the belligerent's service before the commencement of the war" (art. 23 HC IV).

2. Protocols Additional to the Geneva Conventions (1977 and 2005)

a. *Protocols Additional I and II (1977)*

Two additional Protocols to the 1949 Geneva Conventions were adopted in 1977 to strengthen the protection of victims of international and non-international armed conflicts:

- Protocol Additional to the Geneva Conventions of 12 August 1949, and relating to the Protection of Victims of International Armed Conflicts (Protocol I), 8 June 1977 (entry into force 7 December 1979); and
- Protocol Additional to the Geneva Conventions of 12 August 1949, and relating to the Protection of Victims of Non-International Armed Conflicts (Protocol II), 8 June 1977 (entry into force 7 December 1979).

Protocol I, dealing with international armed conflicts, is thorough and detailed, while Protocol II, dealing with non-international armed conflicts, is brief. The Protocols place limits on the conduct of states during hostilities, the use of weapons of war, and the ways wars are fought.

In the two decades following the adoption of the 1949 Geneva Conventions, there was an increase in the number of non-international armed conflicts and wars of national liberation. Protocol II was adopted to establish rules governing conduct in such conflicts. Whereas common article 3 of the Geneva Conventions was the first codification of the rules of non-international conflict, Protocol II was the first international treaty devoted exclusively to non-international armed conflicts.

b. *Protocol Additional III (2005)*

Protocol additional to the Geneva Conventions of 12 August 1949, and relating to the Adoption of an Additional Distinctive Emblem (Protocol III) was adopted on 8 December 2005 and entered into force on 14 January 2006. It created an additional emblem—"a red frame in the shape of a square on edge on a white ground – commonly referred to as the red crystal." The red crystal is intended to provide a further option to and has the same international status as the red cross and red crescent emblems.

3. Other Conventions

A range of other conventions and protocols covering areas such as conventional weapons, chemical weapons, landmines, laser weapons, cluster munitions, and the protection of children in armed conflicts have been adopted by the international community.

a. *Convention on Certain Conventional Weapons (1980)*

The UN Convention on Prohibitions or Restrictions on the Use of Certain Conventional Weapons Which May be Deemed to be Excessively Injurious or to Have Indiscriminate Effects (Geneva, October 10, 1980; 113 State parties), colloquially known as the "Convention on Conventional Weapons" (CCW), as its title suggests, seeks to prohibit or restrict the use of conventional weapons considered to be excessively injurious or to have indiscriminate effects.

The Convention contains the following five Protocols:

- *Protocol (I) on Non-Detectable Fragments* (adopted on October 10, 1980, in Geneva; 111 State parties). Prohibits the use of any weapon whose primary effect is to injure by fragments that escape detection by X-rays in the human body.

- *Protocol (II) on Prohibitions or Restrictions on the Use of Mines, Booby-Traps and Other Devices* (adopted on October 10, 1980, in Geneva; 94 State parties). Restricts landmines and booby traps and deals with marking minefields and removing mines at the end of a conflict. The United States and a number of other countries amended the Protocol on May 3, 1996, to require anti-personnel land mines (APMs) outside marked minefields to self-detonate within a limited time and to forbid non-detectable APLs.

- *Protocol (III) on Prohibitions or Restrictions on the Use of Incendiary Weapons* (adopted on October 10, 1980, in Geneva; 108 State parties). Restricts incendiary weapons in certain instances.

- *Protocol (IV) on Blinding Laser Weapons* (adopted on October 13, 1995, in Vienna; 98 State parties). Restricts the use of weapons specifically designed to cause permanent blindness to unenhanced vision.

- Protocol (V) on Explosive Remnants of War (adopted on November 28, 2003 in Geneva; 69 State parties). Sets out obligations and best practice for the clearance of explosive remnants of war.

b. *Chemical Weapons Convention (1993)*

The 1993 Convention on the Prohibition of the Development, Production, Stockpiling and Use of Chemical Weapons and on their Destruction, colloquially known as the "Chemical Weapons Convention," entered into force 29 April 1997. It bans the use of all chemical weapons and of riot control agents "as a method of warfare." The Convention complements the 1925 Geneva Gas Protocol, but is different in some respects. For example, whereas the 1925 Protocol allows parties to reserve their right to to use chemical weapons in response to a "first use" against them, the 1993 Convention does not allow such reservations. Furthermore, while the 1925 Protocol applies only to international armed conflicts between the parties, the 1993 Convention applies to both international and internal armed conflicts.

c. *Ottawa Convention (1997)*

The Convention on the Prohibition of the Use, Stockpiling, Production and Transfer of Anti-Personnel Mines and on their Destruction (1997), colloquially known as the Ottawa Treaty or the Mine Ban Treaty (MBT), completely bans all anti-personnel mines (APMs). At present, 156 states are parties to the treaty. The US declined to sign the treaty because it would have required removal of US minefields along the Korean border, which the US views as a major deterrent to a North Korean attack.

VI. INTERNATIONAL CRIMINAL LAW

A. Introduction and Definitions

International criminal law deals with the prohibition and punishment of international crimes, which can be defined as internationally wrongful acts resulting from breaches by a state, state agent, or non-state actor of peremptory norms (*jus cogens*) so essential for the protection of the international community's fundamental interests that the breach is classified by the community as a crime. Examples of international crimes include aggression, torture, and genocide. Individuals may be held responsible for violations of international criminal law whether they are acting as state agents with a nexus to state action or as non-state actors with no such nexus.

B. State Actors and Non-State Actors Compared

1. State Actors

State actors are those acting with a nexus to state action. Criminal responsibility may be placed on individual state actors under international law. As an example, we may consider the Nuremberg trials under the 1945 London Charter for the International Military Tribunal. At the time, individual criminal responsibility for violations of international law was a novel idea, yet the Nuremberg Tribunal held that "crimes against international law are committed by men, not by abstract entities, and only by punishing individuals who commit such crimes can the provisions of international law be enforced."

On this basis, the IMT prosecuted state individual actors for crimes against humanity, crimes against peace (aggression), and war crimes. All of the defendants had a nexus with state action because they were Nazi officials or private industrialists with a nexus to Nazi state action.

The IMT did not, however, address the question of whether international law could be violated by non-state actors, but this question would be examined by subsequent tribunals.

2. Non-State Actors

With the increased recognition of non-state actors as violators of international law, there has been renewed and increasing interest in assigning responsibility and accountability to them for their actions. There has thus been a trend in both domestic as well as international law to find jurisdiction in such cases.

a. Domestic Courts: the Case of Kadic v. Karadzic (US Ct. App. 1995)

As an example of this trend, we can consider the case *Kadic v. Karadzic* (US Ct. App. 1995), where the US Second Circuit Court examined the individual criminal responsibility of Karadzic, the leader of the territory of Srpska, one of the two administrative divisions of Bosnia and Herzegovina, and whether he can be sued civilly in the US under the Alien Tort Claims Act (ATCA), which allows suit to be brought in US federal courts by aliens for torts committed outside of the US "in violation of the law of nations or a treaty of the United States" (28 USC 1350). By "law of nations," the statute is referring to international law comprised not only of international treaties, but also international customary law and the general principles of law. Most of the alleged violations of international law are international crimes, and the court assumed that if these offenses are crimes under international law, they are also the basis of a civil suit under the ATCA.

The court dealt with the question of whether a private non-state actor could commit crimes against humanity, genocide, and war crimes. The Nuremberg Tribunal did not answer these questions because all of defendants were Nazi officials or private industrialists with a nexus to Nazi state action. The court held that crimes against humanity, genocide, and war crimes *can* be committed by non-state actors: "We do not agree that the law of nations, as understood in the modern era, confines its reach to state action. Instead, we hold that certain forms of conduct violate the law of nations whether undertaken by those acting under the auspices of a state or only as private individuals." The Court cited the RFR in defending its position:

> "Individuals may be held liable for offenses against international law, such as piracy, war crimes, and genocide." Restatement (Third) pt. II, introductory note. The Restatement is careful to identify those violations that are actionable when committed by a state, Restatement (Third) § 702, [FN3] and a more limited category of violations of "universal concern," id. § 404, [FN4] partially overlapping with those listed in section 702. Though the immediate focus of section 404 is to identify those offenses for which a state has jurisdiction to punish without regard to territoriality or the nationality of the offenders, cf. id. § 402(1)(a), (2), the inclusion of piracy and slave trade from an earlier era and aircraft hijacking from the modern era demonstrates that the offenses of "universal concern" include those capable of being committed by non-state actors.

The appeals court thus reversed the district court's dismissal and permitted the case to move forward on the merits.

b. Accountability in International Courts

While the London Charter's definition of crimes against humanity could potentially apply to persecution by non-state actors, the ICTY and ICTR made clear that such persecution could be committed by such actors, with the ICTY actually convicting a number of non-state actors for crimes against humanity.

The ICC similarly allows prosecutions of individual non-state actors. In defining "crimes against humanity," the SICC requires that attacks directed against any civilian population involve a "course of conduct involving the multiple commission [of murder, extermination, enslavement, etc., mentioned in paragraph 1] against any civilian population, pursuant to or in furtherance of a State or organizational policy to commit such attack" (art. 7.2 SICC). Thus, by including "organizational policy," the SICC was contemplating acts by organizations, such as insurrection movements or other groups that may not have a clear nexus with state action.

C. International Criminal Courts

Violations of international criminal law may be prosecuted by independent international courts, such as the ICC, as well as *ad hoc* international criminal courts created by the Security Council, such as the International Criminal Tribunal for the Former Yugoslavia, or by select members of the international community, such as the Nuremberg International Military Tribunal, which investigate and prosecute crimes within a certain territory and during a certain time.

1. The International Criminal Court

a. Overview

The International Criminal Court (ICC), based at The Hague, is the first permanent, treaty based, international criminal court established to help end impunity for the perpetrators of serious crimes of concern to the international community. The ICC is an independent international organization, and is not part of the United Nations system. Although the Court's expenses are funded primarily by State parties, it also receives voluntary contributions from governments, international organizations, individuals, corporations, and other entities.

The Statute of the ICC ("Rome Statute") established and governs the ICC. It was adopted at a diplomatic conference in Rome in 1998 and entered into force in 2002. At present, 111 states are party to the statute, and a further 38 states have signed the treaty but have not ratified it.

b. Jurisdiction

Under article 5 SICC, the Court has jurisdiction over the following crimes:

- *Genocide*. Defined as any of the following acts committed on members of any national, ethnical, religious or racial group with the intent to destroy it: killing, causing of serious bodily or mental harm, prevention of birth, transferring of children to another group, or infliction of conditions of life calculated to bring about its physical destruction (art. 6 SICC);

- *Crimes against humanity*. Certain enumerated inhuman and odious acts committed as part of a systematic attack against any civilian population that constitute grave humiliation or degradation or a serious attack on human dignity. The SICC enumerates a series of crimes, including murder, extermination, and enslavement, that constitute crimes against humanity when "committed as part of a widespread or systematic attack directed against any civilian population, with knowledge of the attack" (art. 7.1 SICC).

- *War crimes*. Defined by the Geneva Conventions as a criminal violation or grave breach of International humanitarian law (the law of war). The SICC provides an extensive list of examples of war crimes under its jurisdiction, including the willful killing murder or ill-treatment of the sick, the wounded, or prisoners of war; torture and inhuman treatment; extensive destruction not justified by military necessity; the taking of hostages; plunder of public or private property; intentionally directing attacks against civilians or civilian objects including cities, towns, and villages; pillaging a town or village; and the employment of poisoned weapons, among others (art. 8 SICC).

- *Aggression*. Also termed "crime against peace," it is generally defined under customary international law and the Nuremberg Principles as the planning, preparation, initiation, or waging of any war in violation of international law, treaties, or agreements, including participation, conspiracy or complicity in the same (*see* Nuremberg Principles VI and VII). However, because the crime of aggression has not been defined in the SICC, the ICC will not prosecute it until a precise definition has been adopted (art. 5.2 SICC).

An important exception to the foregoing are defensive military actions taken under Article 51 of the UN Charter. Such defensive actions are subject to immediate Security Council review, but do not require UN permission to be legal within international law. "Nothing in the present Charter shall impair the inherent right of individual or collective self-defence if an armed attack occurs against a Member of the United Nations." (UN Charter, Article 51) The Security Council will determine if the action is legally the "right of individual or collective self-defence", or it may appoint another UN organ to do this.

A State which becomes a party to the Rome Statute accepts the jurisdiction of the ICC with respect to these crimes (art. 12.1 SICC). The Court may exercise its jurisdiction if one of the following preconditions occurs:

- One or more of the following states are parties to the Rome Statute: "(a) The State on the territory of which the conduct in question occurred or, if the crime was committed on board a vessel or aircraft, the State of registration of that vessel or aircraft; (b) The State of which the person accused of the crime is a national" (art. 12.2 SICC); or

- One of the states mentioned in the preceding paragraph, if not party to the SICC, yet its acceptance is required under art. 12.2 SICC, that state, by declaration lodged with the Registrar, accepts "the exercise of jurisdiction by the Court with respect to the crime in question" (art. 12.3 SICC).

Thus, in order for the ICC to exercise jurisdiction, the crime must have been committed in the territory of a member state or on board a vessel or aircraft registered with a member state or the state of the accused must be a member state or otherwise, the state in question must agree to jurisdiction.

Once one of these preconditions occur, the Court may exercise jurisdiction if: (a) a crime over which the ICC appears to have jurisdiction is referred to the prosecutor of the ICC by a state party, according to article 14 SICC; or by (b) the Security Council acting under chapter VII of the CUN; or (c) the prosecutor of the ICC has initiated an investigation *proprio motu* with respect to such a crime in accordance with article 15 SICC on the basis of information received from individuals or organizations (art. 13 SICC). In the case of an investigation *propio motu*, the Prosecutor must submit to the Pre-Trial Chamber a request for authorization of an investigation and the Pre-Trial Chamber must find a reasonable basis to proceed with an investigation (art. 15.2-.3 SICC).

Thus, individual victims to alleged international crimes may only have their cases heard only if their state prosecutors refer the crime to the prosecutor of the ICC, the SC refers the case to the ICC, or otherwise, the prosecutor of the ICC initiates an investigation *propio motu*.

Nationals of a country may be prosecuted if (i) the country has ratified the Statute of the ICC; or (ii) they committed a crime while in the territory of a country that ratified the treaty.

c. Rights of the Accused

The SICC includes a long list of due process rights of the accused.

These include, among others, the right to be present at the trial, to conduct the defense in person or through legal assistance of the accused's choosing, to have legal assistance assigned by the Court and without payment if the accused lacks sufficient means to pay for it, to confront witnesses against him, and to remain silent (not to be compelled to testify or to confess guilt) (art. 67.1 SICC).

The right to a trial by jury is not set forth in the SICC. Rather, ICC trial verdicts and decisions are made by panels of three judges. This may be in part because of the impracticality of impaneling a jury to hear an international criminal case.

d. Applicable Penalties

The maximum penalty that can be imposed by the ICC is life imprisonment, a fine, and a forfeiture of property derived from the crime. Under the SICC, subject to review by the Court concerning reduction of sentence, the Court may impose one of the following penalties on a person convicted of genocide, crimes against humanity, war crimes, or the crime of aggression:

"(a)   Imprisonment for a specified number of years, which may not exceed a maximum of 30 years; or

(b) A term of life imprisonment when justified by the extreme gravity of the crime and the individual circumstances of the convicted person.

2. In addition to imprisonment, the Court may order:

(a) A fine under the criteria provided for in the Rules of Procedure and Evidence;

(b) A forfeiture of proceeds, property and assets derived directly or indirectly from that crime, without prejudice to the rights of bona fide third parties" (art. 5.1 SICC).

e. Relationship with the United Nations

As already mentioned, the ICC is an independent international organization that is not part of the UN system. It is legally and functionally independent from the UN. However, the two entities do enjoy a relationship of mutual support. A "Relationship Agreement between the International Criminal Court and the United Nations" governs the ICC's relations with the UN and allows cooperation with the UN in various areas, including the exchange of information and logistical support. The court reports to the UN each year on its activities and some meetings of the Assembly of States Parties are held at UN facilities.

Furthermore, article 13.b of the SICC allows the UN Security Council to refer to the court situations that would not otherwise fall under the court's jurisdiction, as it did in relation to the situation in Darfur, the Sudan. The Sudan holds that the ICC does not have jurisdiction because the preconditions of article 12 SICC were not fulfilled: the alleged crimes took place in and the accused are from the Sudan, which is not a state party to the Rome Treaty. The ICC judges, however, took a more expansive reading of article 13(b) SICC: the SC, acting out of its Chapter VII CUN powers, may refer such cases to the ICC regardless of the preconditions of article 12 SICC.

f. States Parties to the Rome Statute

As of this writing, there were 114 states parties to the Rome Statute: Afghanistan, Albania, Andorra, Antigua and Barbuda, Argentina, Australia, Austria, Bangladesh, Barbados, Belgium, Belize, Benin, Bolivia, Bosnia and Herzegovina, Botswana, Brazil, Bulgaria, Burkina Faso, Burundi, Cambodia, Canada, Central African Republic, Chad, Chile, Colombia, Comoros, Congo, Cook Islands, Costa Rica, Croatia, Cyprus, Czech Republic, Democratic Republic of the Congo, Denmark, Djibouti, Dominica, Dominican Republic, Ecuador , Estonia, Fiji, Finland, France, Gabon, Gambia, Georgia, Germany, Ghana, Greece, Guinea, Guyana, Honduras, Hungary, Iceland, Ireland, Italy, Japan, Jordan, Kenya, Latvia, Lesotho, Liberia, Liechtenstein, Lithuania, Luxembourg, Madagascar, Malawi, Mali, Malta,

Marshall Islands, Mauritius, Mexico, Mongolia, Montenegro, Namibia, Nauru, Netherlands , New Zealand, Niger, Nigeria, Norway, Panama, Paraguay, Peru, Poland, Portugal, Republic of Korea, Republic of Moldova, Romania, Saint Kitts and Nevis, Saint Lucia, Saint Vincent and the Grenadines, Samoa, San Marino, Senegal, Serbia, Seychelles, Sierra Leone, Slovakia, Slovenia, South Africa, Spain, Suriname, Sweden, Switzerland, Tajikistan, The Former Yugoslav Republic of Macedonia, Timor-Leste, Trinidad and Tobago, Uganda, United Kingdom, United Republic of Tanzania, Uruguay, Venezuela, and Zambia.

2. *Ad Hoc* Tribunals

a. *Nuremberg International Military Tribunal*

The Nuremberg International Military Tribunal (IMT) was a court convened jointly by the victorious Allied governments (American, British, French, and Soviet) in 1945 to adjudicate crimes against the Nazi regime. The Tribunal proceeded according to the laws and procedures set out by the London Charter of the International Military Tribunal ("London Charter") (LC), issued on August 8, 1945, and adjudicated the following crimes:

- *Crimes against peace (crimes of aggression)*. This was defined in the London Charter as the "planning, preparation, initiation or waging of a war of aggression, or a war in violation of international treaties, agreements or assurances, or participation in a common plan or conspiracy for the accomplishment of any of the foregoing" (art. 6(a) LC).

- *War crimes*. The London Charter defined war crimes as "violations of the laws or customs of war," also known as *jus in bello* or, in contemporary parlance, international humanitarian law, which regulates the conduct of war (art. 6(b) LC). For the specifics of these crimes, the Allies drew upon the customary laws of war, the Geneva Conventions of 1864, 1906, and 1929, and the Hague Conventions of 1899 and 1907 dealing with the methods and weapons of war. The court was granted jurisdiction to try "murder, ill-treatment or deportation to slave labor or for any other purpose of civilian population of or in occupied territory, murder or ill-treatment of prisoners of war or persons on the seas, killing of hostages, plunder of public or private property, wanton destruction of cities, towns or villages, or devastation not justified by military necessity," all of which constitute violations of the laws of war (art. 6(b) LC).

- *Crimes against humanity*. These are enumerated inhuman and odious acts committed as part of a systematic attack against any civilian population. For the purposes of the IMT, crimes against humanity included "murder, extermination, enslavement, deportation, and other inhumane acts," as well as "persecutions on political, racial or religious grounds" (art. 6(c) LC). The Nazis were responsible for crimes against humanity committed against their own citizens.

Genocide was not prosecuted because it had not as of yet been defined in the London Charter. The Convention on the Prevention and Punishment of the Crime of Genocide was concluded three years later in 1948.

b. *International Military Tribunal for the Far East*

At the conclusion of WWII, Asian countries victimized by Japanese aggression tried thousands of Japanese for war crimes in their own courts. As many as 900 Japanese were executed and many more were sentenced to life in prison.

In addition to these domestic courts, which found jurisdiction on the basis of crimes committed by the Japanese on the Asian nations' own territory or against their own people, the US military established the International Military Tribunal for the Far East (IMTFE), also known as the Tokyo Trials or the Tokyo War Crimes Tribunal, to try the leaders of the Empire of Japan for the following crimes:

- "Class A" crimes, charging 28 Japanese military and political leaders in the highest decision-making bodies who participated in a joint conspiracy to start and wage war;
- "Class B" crimes, charging thousands of Japanese nationals who committed "conventional" atrocities or crimes against humanity;
- "Class C" crimes, charging thousands of Japanese for the planning, ordering, authorization, or failure to prevent such transgressions at higher levels of command.

The Charter of the IMTFE followed generally the model set by the Nuremberg Trials. Like the IMT, the IMTFE charged defendants for crimes against peace (aggression), crimes against humanity, and conventional war crimes (violations of IHL).

c. International Criminal Tribunal for the Former Yugoslavia (ICTY)

The Chapter VII powers of the SC enables members to move quickly in order to end a conflict threatening international peace. In the 1990s, violence in the Balkans was destabilizing the region. The international community chose to act quickly through the SC in creating the ICTY, rather than through negotiating a treaty that could take a great deal of time and whose enforcements states could avoid by refusing to ratify the treaty. In acting through a Chapter VII resolution, the SC was able to bind all UN members.

In 1993, SC established the International Criminal Tribunal for the Former Yugoslavia (ICTY) to prosecute those responsible for committing war crimes and genocide. The ICTY set a precedent by convicting a number of non-state actors for crimes against humanity. Successful convictions of these political and military leaders were meant to bring justice to victims and deter others from committing such crimes in the future.

The ICTY Statute grants jurisdiction to try the following crimes that occurred in the territory of the former Yugoslavia beginning in 1991: (i) crimes against humanity; (ii) genocide, which evolved as a crime against humanity, but now has its own distinct definition; and (iii) war crimes, including grave breaches of the Geneva Conventions as well as other violations of the laws of war based in either treaties or custom.

d. International Criminal Tribunal for Rwanda (ICTR)

The United Nations also established a special international criminal tribunal in Rwanda to prosecute those responsible for committing genocide and war crimes. Like the ICTY, the Rwanda Tribunal was meant to bring justice to victims and to deter others from committing such crimes in the future.

The major difference between the ICTY and ICTR is that the Rwandan conflict was domestic, whereas the Yugoslavian conflict became international when Yugoslavia dissolved into several independent states. In both cases, the SC acted pursuant to its Chapter VII powers to create the ICTR to try the following crimes that occurred in the territory of Rwanda within the 1994 calendar year: (i) crimes against humanity; (ii) genocide; and (iii) war crimes (we see only common article 3 and Protocol 2 of the Geneva Conventions, because this conflict was internal).

e. Special Court for Sierra Leone

The Special Court for Sierra Leone (SCSL) is an independent judicial body based in Freetown set up by a treaty between Sierra Leone and the UN to try those who bear greatest responsibility for the war crimes and crimes against humanity committed in Sierra Leone after 30 November 1996 during the Sierra Leone Civil War. Among the indictees is former Liberian president Charles Taylor, who was heavily involved with the civil war in Sierra Leone.

The Court seeks to bring justice for violations of common article 3 of the Geneva Conventions and its Protocol Additional II, both of which deal with conflicts not of an international nature, as well as for serious violations of Sierra Leonean criminal law.

f. Human Rights Chamber for Bosnia & Herzegovina

The Human Rights Chamber for Bosnia and Herzegovina served as a judicial body established in Bosnia and Herzegovina within Annex 6 to the General Framework Agreement for Peace in Bosnia and Herzegovina (Dayton Peace Agreement), which was reached at Wright-Patterson Air Force Base near Dayton, Ohio in November 1995, and signed in Paris in December 1995.

The Human Rights Chamber operated between 1996 and 2003 with the mandate to consider alleged or apparent violations of human rights as provided in the European Convention for the Protection of Human Rights and Fundamental Freedoms and the Protocols thereto, and alleged or apparent discrimination arising in the enjoyment of the rights and freedoms provided for in the Convention and 15 other international agreements listed in the Appendix to Annex 6 of the Dayton Peace Agreement. Particular priority was given to allegations of especially severe or systematic violations, as well as those founded on alleged discrimination on prohibited grounds.

The Chamber was receiving applications concerning such human rights violations directly from any Party to Annex 6 of the Dayton Peace Agreement or from any person, non-governmental organisation or group of individuals claiming to be the victim of a violation by any Party or acting on behalf of alleged victims who are deceased or missing.

g. Special Tribunal for Lebanon

The Special Tribunal for Lebanon (STL) is an international criminal tribunal based in Leidschendam-Voorburg, near The Hague, established with a UN Security Council mandate of investigating and prosecuting, under international law, criminal acts relating to the assassination of former Lebanese Prime Minister Rafiq Hariri and the killing of 22 others in the attack of February 14, 2005.

On 13 December 2005, the Republic of Lebanon requested that the UN establish an international tribunal to try all those allegedly responsible for the attack of 14 February 2005 in Beirut. The Tribunal was established by an agreement between the UN and the Lebanese Republic pursuant to SC resolution 1664 (2006) of 29 March 2006. The United Nations

Security Council, acting under Chapter VII of the CUN, endorsed the agreement on 30 May 2007 (SC Resolution 1757 (2007)).

3. The International Criminal Court and *Ad Hoc* Tribunals Compared

The main difference between the ICC and the *ad hoc* tribunals is that while the *ad hoc* tribunals are created as temporary tribunals with jurisdiction to try certain crimes that took place within a certain territory at a certain time, the ICC is a permanent institution that has much broader jurisdiction. It may try any crime committed within the territory of any state party to the SICC or on board a vessel or aircraft if the vessel or aircraft was registered with a state party to the SICC, or if the crime was committed against victims of a state party to the ICC, or otherwise, when the acceptance of a state not party to the SICC is a necessary precondition to the ICC's jurisdiction and that state accepts the ICC's jurisdiction (art. 12 SICC).

As a further difference between the ICC and the *ad hoc* tribunals, while the ICC was created by a multilateral treaty that binds only those states parties to it, the *ad hoc* tribunals were created by SC resolutions that are binding on all member states.

VII. HUMAN RIGHTS AND RELATED TOPICS

A. Human Rights Law and the Principle of Nonintervention

1. Introduction

One phenomenon that has led to rapid developments in international law and the structure of the international legal system is the increased and nearly universal recognition of the protection of human rights as a proper concern of international law. As mentioned earlier in the definition section, international law may govern not only the relationships between states and international organizations *inter se*, but also, some of their relations with natural persons. Human rights is one of the principal areas where the relationships of individuals to states is governed by international law. Individual victims of human rights, rather the states corresponding to their nationality, may in some international legal institutions bring forth claims against the alleged violating states, as is the case of the ECHR. Other international courts, such as the ICC, do not permit individuals to bring suit directly against states, but they offer individuals protection by permitting their states of nationality to refer cases to the ICC.

In this same spirit, various human rights instruments have been interpreted to permit prosecutions of conduct committed by individuals, including even non-state actors. Perhaps the best example is the Statute of the ICC, which implies in article 7.2 that non-state organizations with a policy of directing attacks towards civilians may be prosecuting by the ICC.

2. Principle of Nonintervention

It is a principle of customary international law that states and international organizations may not interfere or intervene in matters within the domestic jurisdiction of other states. The CUN recognizes this principle when it states: "Nothing contained in the present Charter shall authorize the United Nations to intervene in matters which are essentially within the domestic jurisdiction of any state or shall require the Members to submit such matters to settlement under the present Charter" (art. 2.7 CUN). Thus, states traditionally could act with immunity in their domestic affairs, even if in doing so, the human rights of their own people were violated. International law would only apply when nationals of other countries would fall victims to the crimes of a state.

After WWII, however, practice departed from this precedent with the establishment of the Nuremberg International Military Tribunal, which was established by the London Charter and adjudicated the Nazi regime's crimes against its own people. Since then, international human rights law has ignored the principle of nonintervention for the most egregious crimes, and states are obliged under their human rights treaties to respect the rights of both their citizens as well as aliens within their borders, and other states or international organizations may intervene to assure that these rights are respected if a state fails to take action to protect them. The CUN incorporates this premise when articulating an exception to the general rule of sovereignty: the principle of nonintervention "shall not prejudice the application of enforcement measures under Chapter VII [of the Charter]" (art. 2.7 CUN).

The development of this principle was largely influenced by the atrocities committed in WWII. The Allied Powers would not let the authorities responsible for war crimes by German and Japanese authorities, and particularly those committed against their own citizens, go free through the application of the principle of nonintervention, as doing so would be a miscarriage of justice. Under this exception to the principle of nonintervention, the IMT and IMTFE were established to try Nazi Germany and Imperial Japan's war crimes.

B. Sources of International Human Rights Law

Because human rights law is primarily treaty-based, states not party to human rights treaties are not bound by them. However, treaties that have been universally or nearly universally adopted may become sources of customary international law binding even over groups that have not formally accepted their terms.

Human rights law is also partially contained in non-codified customary international law as well as in non-binding international declarations. It may also be contained in general principles of law.

In the domestic sphere, human rights, often termed "civil rights," is governed by statutes or by constitutional guarantees, as is the case of England, the US, and France.

1. Origins of Human Rights Law in Domestic Law

Human rights has developed, first in domestic law, from as early as the English *Magna Carta*, which is widely accepted to be the "mother document" of human rights instruments. In response to abuses under King John's tyrannical rule and application of the principle *Rex Lex* (the king is the law), English barons revolted and forced the King to sign the *Magna Carta* in 1215 to protect citizens' rights and the principle of the rule of law (*Lex Rex*—the law is king). The *Magna Carta* established the freedom of the Church to be free from the interference of the king, the protection of private property, *habeas corpus*, due process in civil and criminal proceedings, and taxation by consent.

From the *Magna Carta* came other developments in English law that would ultimately have an international influence in nations such as the US and France. With tensions under King Charles I rising, the Upper and Lower Houses of Parliament eventually conditioned their cooperation with Charles in raising taxes on the king's signing of the 1628 Petition of Right, which was drawn up by Edward Coke to protect rights including *taxation only with representation and the prohibition of arbitrary imprisonment*. It also protected the rule of law and petitioned the king to remove stationed soldiers and mariners who obliged the citizens to receive them into their homes. The Glorious Revolution in England gave way to the Declaration of Rights and Liberties of the Subject, which would in 1689 be enacted as a statute entitled the "Bill of Rights," which echoed many of the elements of the Petition of Right in 1628 under King Charles, such as the prohibition of taxation without representation and of standing armies in times of peace. The list of enumerated rights also set limitations on royal power.

The English Bill of Rights foreshadowed and, to an extent, inspired the American Bill of Rights, which were introduced to the first US Congress in 1789 as a series of legislative articles, and came into effect as Constitutional Amendments in 1791, through the process of ratification by three-fourths of the States. The US Bill of Rights, among its other provisions, limits the powers of the federal government, guarantees freedom of religion, freedom of speech and of the press, free assembly and free association, the right to bear arms, the right to a speedy trial with an impartial jury, the right not to be forced to testify against oneself, and due process under law, and reserves for the people any rights not specifically enumerated in the Constitution.

The French model in some ways follows this same tradition. In France, the Declaration of the Rights of Man and of the Citizen, adopted in 1791, serves as a bill of rights that defines man's rights to "liberty, property, security and resistance to oppression." It called for the destruction of aristocratic privileges and the restriction of the monarchy, and a popular sovereignty with all citizens taking part. Freedom of speech and press were declared, arbitrary arrests were outlawed, and the rights of man were held to be universally valid at all times and in all places. The French Declaration of the Rights of Man and of the Citizen is seen by many as a precursor to the UN's Universal Declaration of Human Rights.

2. Non-Binding International Declarations

a. *American Declaration of the Rights and Duties of Man (1948)*

The American Declaration of the Rights and Duties of Man (ADRDM) was adopted by the nations of the Americas at the same meeting that created the OAS in 1948—the Ninth International Conference of American States in Bogotá. It was the world's first international human rights instrument and predated the UDHR by less than a year.

The ADRDM is comprised of a preface followed by two chapters: Chapter One on Rights, beginning with the right to life, liberty, and security, and progressing to the rights to equality before the law, religious freedom, expression, and a host of other rights—and Chapter Two on Duties, laying out a series of duties to society and family. These duties include the duty to receive instruction, to vote, to obey the law, to serve the community, to cooperate with the state with respect to social security and welfare, to pay taxes, to work, and to refrain from political activities in other countries.

b. *Universal Declaration of Human Rights (UN 1948)*

The Universal Declaration of Human Rights (UDHR) was adopted by the UN General Assembly on December 10, 1948. Most sources consider the UDHR to be a nonbinding resolution that set forth a "common standard of achievement for all peoples and all nations" (Preamble UDHR). Other sources view it as an elaboration of the human rights provisions of the UN Charter, and thus claim that it is binding through the Charter. Yet others, as mentioned above, consider it to be a source of binding customary international law.

The UDHR was passed by a vote of 48 in favor, zero against, and eight abstentions (Byelorussian SSR, Czechoslovakia, Poland, Ukrainian SSR, USSR, Yugoslavia, South Africa, and Saudi Arabia). The following countries voted in favor of the Declaration: Afghanistan, Argentina, Australia, Belgium, Bolivia, Brazil, Burma, Canada, Chile, China, Colombia, Costa Rica, Cuba, Denmark, the Dominican Republic, Ecuador, Egypt, El Salvador, Ethiopia, France, Greece, Guatemala, Haiti, Iceland, India, Iran, Iraq, Lebanon, Liberia, Luxembourg, Mexico, Netherlands, New Zealand, Nicaragua, Norway, Pakistan, Panama, Paraguay, Peru, Philippines, Thailand, Sweden, Syria, Turkey, United Kingdom, United States, Uruguay and Venezuela.

c. *Cairo Declaration on Human Rights in Islam (1990)*

The Cairo Declaration on Human Rights in Islam (CDHRI) is a declaration of the member states of the Organisation of the Islamic Conference (OIC) adopted in Cairo in 1990, which provides an overview on the Islamic perspective on human rights and affirms Shari'ah as its sole source. The purpose of the CDHRI is "general guidance for Member States [of the OIC] in the Field of human rights." This declaration is usually seen as an Islamic response to the post-World War II UN UDHR of 1948.

3.   Customary International Law

As defined above, customary international law results from a general and consistent practice of states followed by them from a sense of legal obligation. Unlike treaties, which are binding on only states parties thereto, customary law is binding on all states.

Customary international law in the field of human rights may develop primarily as a result of international treaties when they are adopted by a large plurality of states, such that the practices contained therein become general and consistent binding practices in the international arena, as well as when international declarations are widely accepted and practiced by the international community. Some have argued, for example, that the UDHR, though it is a non-binding declaration, has to some extent evolved into a source of binding customary international law because of its wide acceptance and consistent and recurrent practice by states.

4.   Binding International Treaties and Conventions

a.   *United Nations Treaties*

i.   United Nations Charter (1945)

The CUN states that one of the purposes of the UN is to achieve "international co-operation in … promoting and encouraging respect for human rights and for fundamental freedoms for all without distinction as to race, sex, language, or religion" (art. 1.3 CUN). This is reemphasized in article 55, which declares that "the United Nations shall promote … universal respect for, and observance of, human rights and fundamental freedoms for all without distinction as to race, sex, language, or religion" (art. 55 CUN). However, because the only concrete human right expressly mentioned in the Charter is nondiscrimination ("distinction as to race, sex, language, or religion"), members of the UN came together to draft the UDHR (*see supra.*), which more clearly defines the human rights to be protected in the international order. The UDHR, because it is not binding, in turn gave rise to two other instruments: the International Covenant on Civil and Political Rights and the International Covenant on Economic, Social, and Cultural Rights (*see infra.*), both binding instruments.

ii.   Convention on the Prevention and Punishment of the Crime of Genocide (1948)

The Convention on the Prevention and Punishment of the Crime of Genocide (Genocide Convention) was adopted by the UN GA on 9 December, 1948, just one day before the adoption of the Universal Declaration of Human Rights. The Convention, which entered into force in 1951, defines genocide in its second article as:

> any of the following acts committed with intent to destroy, in whole or in part, a national, ethnical, racial or religious group, as such:
> (a) Killing members of the group;
> (b) Causing serious bodily or mental harm to members of the group;
> (c) Deliberately inflicting on the group conditions of life calculated to bring about its physical destruction in whole or in part;
> (d) Imposing measures intended to prevent births within the group;
> (e) Forcibly transferring children of the group to another group.

The Genocide Convention is an example of a human rights instrument that creates an affirmative duty to act. It requires not only that its 140 states parties refrain from the crime of genocide, but also that they "undertake to prevent and to punish" genocide (Art. I CPPG) and further pledge "to grant extradition in accordance with their laws and treaties in force" of persons charged with genocide (Art. VII CPPG). The ICJ thus found in the Bosnian Genocide Case (*Bosnia and Herzegovina v. Serbia and Montenegro*) (2007) that Belgrade breached international law by failing to prevent the 1995 Srebrenica genocide and for failing to try or transfer the persons accused of genocide to the ICTY, in violation of its obligations under the Genocide Convention.

iii. Convention Relating to the Status of Refugees (1951)

The Convention Relating to the Status of Refugees was adopted in 1951 by the United Nations Conference of Plenipotentiaries on the Status of Refugees and Stateless Persons and entered into force in 1954. The Convention is in many ways a human rights convention, in that it seeks to provide protection to any person who owing to "fear of being persecuted for reasons of race, religion, nationality, membership of a particular social group or political opinion, is outside the country of his nationality and is unable, or owing to such fear, is unwilling to avail himself of the protection of that country" (article 1.A(2) CRSR). The CRSR provides such persons the right of asylum in states parties to the Convention and guarantees their rights to favorable conditions for gainful employment and for the practice of the liberal professions, housing, public education, and access to public relief, among other rights.

iv. The International Covenant on Civil and Political Rights (1966) and the International Covenant on Economic, Social and Cultural Rights (1966)

(1) Overview and Comparison

The International Covenant on Civil and Political Rights (ICCPR) and the International Covenant on Economic, Social and Cultural Rights (ICESCR) are two international treaties that aimed at converting the nonbinding provisions of the UDHR into binding treaty provisions. Because the USSR and US were unable to agree as to the rights that should be enumerated (the US argued that economic and social rights do not exist, while the USSR wished to codify them), two separate treaties resulted. Unlike the UDHR, which took only a few years to draft because it was not binding, the drafting of the ICCPR and the ICESCR took 18 years.

Unlike the ICESCR, which the US did not ratify, the ICCPR was signed and ratified by both the US and the USSR. The ICCPR has 154 states parties, while the ICESCR has 151.

(2) International Covenant on Civil and Political Rights (ICCPR)

States parties to the ICCPR, which came into effect on 23 March 1976, undertake to protect the wide range of civil and political rights listed in the ICCPR, including a right to life and prohibitions on torture and slavery. The ICCPR requires states not only to agree to not violate these rights, but also to insure the rights by protecting them from other member states' violations. To guarantee these rights, each state party to the ICCPR is required:

- "(a)   To ensure that any person whose rights or freedoms as herein recognized are violated shall have an effective remedy, notwithstanding that the violation has been committed by persons acting in an official capacity;

- (b)   To ensure that any person claiming such a remedy shall have his right thereto determined by competent judicial, administrative or legislative authorities, or by any other competent authority provided for by the legal system of the State, and to develop the possibilities of judicial remedy;

- (c)   To ensure that the competent authorities shall enforce such remedies when granted" (art. 2(3) ICCPR).

Because there are no specified enforcement mechanisms in the ICCPR, states parties drafted an optional protocol that allows for complaints against violating states to be brought before the eighteen-member Human Rights Committee (HRC), a human rights treaty body with the power to: (i) review reports on compliance submitted by states members to the ICCPR and issue its "Observations"; (ii) issue "General Comments" on the implementation of the ICCPR; and (iii) under the (First) Optional Protocol to the ICCPR, the HRC may consider petitions from individuals claiming to be victims of violations of the ICCPR by a state party to the Convention if the individuals have exhausted the available domestic remedies. The HRC may study the matter and then send its views to the petitioner and to the state, but its views are not binding and only hold the weight of the "views" of the Committee.

(3) International Covenant on Economic, Social and Cultural Rights (ICESCR)

The ICESCR took effect on 3 January 1976 and includes a series of economic rights, including the right to work and join trade unions. States parties agree to the "progressive realization" of these rights. There is thus an affirmative obligation to *take steps* "to the maximum of its available resources" toward the progressive realization of these rights.

v.   Convention on the Elimination of All Forms of Racial Discrimination (1966)

The International Convention on the Elimination of All Forms of Racial Discrimination (ICERD) is a UN convention that was adopted in 1966 and entered into force in 1969. It commits its members to the elimination of racial discrimination and the promotion of understanding among all races.

The Convention includes an individual complaints mechanism, making it enforceable against its parties. The human rights treaty body charged with monitoring and implementing the Convention is the Committee on the Elimination of Racial Discrimination (CERD), which in many ways parallels the mechanisms and procedures of the HRC.

vi. Convention on the Elimination of All Forms of Discrimination Against Women (1979)

The Convention on the Elimination of all Forms of Discrimination against Women (CEDAW) is an international convention adopted by the UN GA in 1979 and entering into force in 1981. It is often described as an "international bill of rights for women." It is a nearly universal convention, with only 7 UN member states that have not ratified it: Iran, Nauru, Palau, Somalia, Sudan, Tonga, and the United States. The implementation of the Convention is monitored by the Committee on the Elimination of Discrimination Against Women (CEDAW), which parallels the mechanisms and procedures of the HRC.

vii. Indigenous and Tribal Peoples Convention (1989)

The Indigenous and Tribal Peoples Convention, an ILC Convention (ILO-convention 169) adopted in 1989 and entering into force in 1991, sets out to guarantee the rights of indigenous peoples, adopt international standards for indigenous peoples with a view to removing the assimilationist orientation of earlier standards, and guarantee indigenous peoples the right to control their own institutions, ways of life and economic development, while maintaining and developing their "identities, languages and religions, within the framework of the States in which they live" (Preamble).

viii.   Convention on the Rights of the Child (1989)

The UN Convention on the Rights of the Child (UNCRC) is a human rights treaty setting out the civil, political, economic, social, and cultural rights of children, defined as any person under the age of eighteen, unless an earlier age of majority is recognized by a country's law. The Convention was adopted in 1989 and became effective in 1990. Its two optional protocols were adopted in 2000.

The Convention and its protocols is monitored by the UN Committee on the Rights of the Child (CRC), which is composed of members from countries around the world. Once a year, the Committee submits a report to the UN GA, which also hears a statement from the CRC Chair, and the GA adopts a Resolution on the Rights of the Child.

b. Regional Treaties

i.   European Convention on Human Rights (1950)

The European Convention on Human Rights, formally known as the Convention for the Protection of Human Rights and Fundamental Freedoms, is an international treaty to protect human rights and fundamental freedoms in Europe. It was drafted in 1950 by the then newly formed Council of Europe and entered into force in 1953. All 47 members of the Council of Europe are parties to the Convention.

ii.   American Convention on Human Rights (1969)

The American Convention on Human Rights (ACHR) (Pact of San José) was adopted by the nations of the Americas meeting in San José, Costa Rica, in 1969, and entered into force in 1978. The ACHR sets out to guarantee a "system of personal liberty and social justice based on respect for the essential rights of man" (Preamble ACHR). It is implemented by the Inter-American Commission on Human Rights and the Inter-American Court of Human Rights, both of which are organs of the OAS that are responsible for overseeing compliance with the ACHR. At present, 11 of the 35 OAS member states, including the US, Canada, and the Republic of Trinidad and Tobago, have not ratified the ACHR.

iii. African Charter on Human and Peoples' Rights (1981)

The African Charter on Human and Peoples' Rights was adopted in 1981 with the purpose of promoting and protecting human rights and basic freedoms in Africa. It emerged under the Organization of African Unity (the predecessor of the African Union), which called for a committee of experts to draft a continent-wide human rights instrument. The draft was unanimously approved as the African Charter on Human and Peoples' Rights at the OAU's

1981 Assembly and entered into force in 1986. The Charter goes further than the ICCPR and the ICESCR by providing for certain rights, such as the right to development.

iv. Arab Charter on Human Rights (1994)

The Arab Charter on Human Rights was adopted by the Arab League in 1994 and entered into force in 2008. It reaffirms the principles contained in the CUN, the UDHR, and the ICCPR. The Preamble also reaffirms the Cairo Declaration on Human Rights in Islam (1990), which specifies human rights in the context of a state governed by *Shar'ia*. The Charter recognizes traditional human rights, such as the right to liberty and security of persons, equality of persons before the law, protection of persons from torture, and the right to property, but article 27 allows for restrictions on freedom of religion, thought, and opinion, when imposed by law.

v. Charter of Fundamental Rights of the European Union (2000)

Adopted on 2 October 2000 and ratified on 7 December 2000, the Charter of Fundamental Rights of the European Union (CFREU) encapsulates civic, personal, economic, and social rights of EU citizens and residents. Its content, which covers human dignity, justice, freedom, equality, and child protection, is based on the rights captured in the constitutional and legal traditions of member countries, on the case-law of the ECJ, and on the CPHR and other international human rights agreements. Under the Charter, the EU must act and legislate consistently with the Charter. The EU's courts will strike down EU legislation that contravenes it.

C. Human Rights Treaty Bodies

The major international human rights treaties have created bodies that are responsible for monitoring the implementation of their respective treaties and considering individual complaints or communications. These bodies, created by the treaties that they monitor, are called "human rights treaty bodies" and are comprised of committees of independent experts. There are nine human rights treaty bodies, all of which receive secretariat support from the Human Rights Treaties Branch of the OHCHR:

- The Human Rights Committee (HRC), perhaps the most prominent of human rights treaty bodies, monitors implementation of the ICCPR (1966) and its optional protocols;
- The Committee on Economic, Social and Cultural Rights (CESCR) monitors implementation of the ICESCR (1966);
- The Committee on the Elimination of Racial Discrimination (CERD) monitors implementation of the International Convention on the Elimination of All Forms of Racial Discrimination (1965);
- The Committee on the Elimination of Discrimination Against Women (CEDAW) monitors implementation of the Convention on the Elimination of All Forms of Discrimination against Women (1979) and its optional protocol (1999);
- The Committee Against Torture (CAT) monitors implementation of the Convention against Torture and Other Cruel, Inhuman or Degrading Treatment (1984);

- The Committee on the Rights of the Child (CRC) monitors implementation of the Convention on the Rights of the Child (1989) and its optional protocols (2000);

- The Committee on Migrant Workers (CMW) monitors implementation of the International Convention on the Protection of the Rights of All Migrant Workers and Members of Their Families (1990);

- The Committee on the Right of Persons with Disabilities (CRPD) monitors implementation of the International Convention on the Rights of Persons with Disabilities (2006); and

- The Committee on Enforced Disappearance (CED) monitors implementation of the International Convention for the Protection of All Persons from Enforced Disappearance (2006).

One mechanism that almost all human rights treaty bodies have is requiring states to periodically submit reports explaining how they are working to fulfill the terms of the respective treaty. After the submission, the treaty bodies give the reports "concluding observations." While these observations may serve as important leverage in the international arena, states are not required to act on them.

D. Remedies for Human Rights Breaches

1. Domestic Remedies

Some nations also allow their residents to bring suit against them in their own domestic courts for civil rights abuses and other wrongs committed by the state or by state actors. Such suits are brought under some form of legislation whereby the state partially waives its immunity to be sued and permits human rights violations (often called "civil rights abuses") to be heard against the state or its agents in its courts. Such legislation may include protection from discrimination, hate crimes, damage to property or to other rights. (For specific examples of national legislations that permit citizens to sue the state or state actors in cases alleging not only human rights abuses, but ordinary torts and criminal cases as well, see Chapter 8 – State Responsibility and Immunities from Jurisdiction, "Partial Waivers of Sovereign Immunity in Domestic Courts," below.)

As a further protection of human rights provided under domestic laws, we may consider asylum laws. Most countries are parties to the CRSR and thus have incorporated asylum laws into their domestic legislation that permit resident aliens to remain in country if the aliens can show that persecution due to race, political views, religious affiliation, or civic membership would result in the resident's home country if he or she were to return. For further treatment on this topic, see "Refugee Law," below.

2. Remedies within the International Framework

A variety of remedies under international law are available for victims of human rights breaches. The remedies depend to a large extent on whether a state or individual committed the violation: states may be required to pay compensation to victims or to change domestic law; individuals may be required to pay a fine or may face criminal penalties, such as imprisonment. In either case, international treaties normally require individuals to have exhausted the domestic remedies available before bringing suit in the international forum (*see, e.g.*, art. 41(1)(c) ICCPR). This requirement is, however, waived if it can be shown that doing so would be unreasonable, ineffective, or the remedy inadequate.

a. Human Rights Violations by Individuals

Until recently, individuals were not seen as subjects or objects of international law, but this has changed beginning with the Nuremberg IMT and later with the IMTFE, both of which tried and convicted a number of state actors for violations of international law.

In the 1990s, the concept was taken further with the ICTY and ICTR, which operated under the understanding that even non-state actors could be held responsible for violations of international law (the ICTY actually convicted a number of such actors).

As yet another international criminal justice mechanism, we may point to the ICC. The ICC has potentially worldwide jurisdiction as long as the perpetrator is a national of a state party or if the persecutory act was committed on the territory of a state party or on a vessel or aircraft registered with a state party. The ICC is empowered not only to prosecute the perpetrator, but also to provide reparations to victims.

b. Human Rights Violations by States

The various human rights regimes have established monitoring mechanisms that are capable of providing varying degrees of redress to victims. The focus of such mechanisms is the responsibility of the state and its obligation to make reparations for human rights violations suffered by victims. Such reparations may encompass a range of measures, including amendment of domestic law, prosecution of perpetrators, and rehabilitation and compensation of victims.

i. Human Rights Treaty Bodies

States may be called to account for violations of human rights by human rights treaty bodies, such as the Human Rights Committee, which are created by human rights treaties to implement and enforce the provisions contained therein. These bodies may receive complaints by individuals or groups of individuals alleging violations of human rights norms by states or by state actors. The human rights treaty bodies may investigate these complaints and make their views known and recommend to states how shortfalls with respect to human rights should be addressed.

ii. International Courts

When domestic remedies are unavailable, or when they have been exhausted, the alleged wrong party may sometimes find recourse in international tribunals. Some of these tribunals, such as the Inter-American Court of Human Rights, are open to individuals, groups of individuals, or NGOs. They generally require the petitioner to show that all domestic remedies have been exhausted before allowing the case to move forward in their courts.

Like domestic remedies, international remedies are only open to citizens or residents of those states that allow themselves to be sued in international tribunals (universal jurisdiction, which applies to the most egregious of crimes, such as genocide, allows the courts of any nation to try nationals of any other nation without the consent of the latter nation, but this is an exception to the general rule). This partial waiver of sovereign immunity is usually achieved through international treaties among nations agreeing to create an international forum for hearing human rights abuse cases, such as the European Court of Human Rights. Only states parties to the treaties may be sued.

For examples of such treaties, we may point to the American Convention of Human Rights, which allows individuals to bring petitions to the Inter-American Commission on Human Rights for human rights violations by OAS member states of the ADRDM or the ACHR. The Commission may in turn refer the case to the Inter-American Court of Human Rights for adjudication. This is similarly the case of the European Convention of Human Rights, which allows individuals to bring cases to the European Court of Human Rights for human rights violations by states parties.

E. Refugee Law

1. Introduction

After World War II, the international community was faced with the task of organizing thousands of displaced persons. There was a concerted effort to ensure that the atrocities committed during the war would never be repeated, and part of this was achieved by adopting the UDHR (1948). In order to secure the fundamental human rights of refugees, the Office of the UN High Commissioner for Refugees (UNHCR) was established on December 14, 1950. Headquartered in Geneva, Switzerland, the agency is mandated with the task of supervising international conventions providing for the protection of refugees. The main principle behind the UNHCR and refugee law in general is to provide surrogate international protection for an individual where national protection of his fundamental rights has failed.

2. UN High Commissioner for Refugees

The primary mission of UNHCR is to promote the protection of refugees. Its role varies greatly from country to country, depending on whether there exists national legislation protecting the rights of refugees, whether there are national agencies or NGOs acting as refugee administrators or whether UNHCR is the primary refugee administrator, and whether UNHCR is even welcome as an international presence. While UNHCR does provide assistance and aid to refugees, its first priority is to advocate for the rights of refugees in host countries. It also encourages the development of national legislation that recognizes the rights of refugees and leads to a fair administration of those rights by national refugee agencies.

The UNHCR may support refugees at the request of states or the UN itself. It assists in the local integration or resettlement of refugees into a third country as well as their voluntary repatriation to their country of origin. The UNHCR has a mandate for internally displaced persons (IDPs), who have had to leave their homes due to persecution, but who are still in their countries of residence; it does not deal with those who have already left their countries of residence.

3. Convention Relating to the Status of Refugees (1967)

a. Introduction

In the year following the establishment of the UNHCR, the main treaty dealing with refugee questions—the 1951 Convention Relating to the Status of Refugees (CRSR), as amended by the 1967 Protocol relating to the Status of Refugees—was adopted. The Convention was approved at a special UN conference on 28 July 1951 and entered into force in 1954. With 147 states parties to either the Convention or its Protocol, the principles contained in the Convention and its Protocol have become part of customary international law.

The Convention is central to the activities of the UNHCR. It defines who is a refugee, sets out their rights, and outlines the responsibilities of the international community in applying protections for refugees.

b. Definition of "Refugee"

Under article 1 of the Convention, as modified by article 1.2 of the Protocol, a refugee is any person who "owing to well-founded fear of being persecuted for reasons of race, religion, nationality, membership of a particular social group or political opinion, is outside the country of his nationality and is unable, or owing to such fear, is unwilling to avail himself of the protection of that country; or who, not having a nationality and being outside the country of his former habitual residence as a result of such events, is unable or, owing to such fear, is unwilling to return to it" (article 1.A(2) CRSR). Several regional conventions have expanded this definition by including persons compelled to leave their country owing to generalized violence (see "Regional Conventions," infra.).

Article 1 also sets out a series of exceptions to the general definition of "refugee" provided above. Even if there is a well-founded fear of persecution for reasons of race, religion, nationality, membership of a social group or political opinion, the following individuals may not seek refugee status:

- An individual who (1) has voluntarily re-availed himself of the protection of the country of his nationality; (2) having lost his nationality, has voluntarily reacquired it; (3) has acquired a new nationality, and enjoys the protection of the country of his new nationality; (4) has voluntarily re-established himself in the country which he left or outside which he remained owing to fear of persecution; or (5) can no longer, because the circumstances in connection with which he has been recognized as a refugee have ceased to exist, continue to refuse to avail himself of the protection of the country of his nationality or is able to return to the country of his former habitual residence (art. 1.C CRSR);

- Persons who are at present receiving from organs or agencies of the UN other than the UNHCR protection or assistance (art. 1.D CRSR);

- A person who is recognized by the competent authorities of the country in which he has taken residence as having the rights and obligations which are attached to the possession of the nationality of that country (art. 1.E CRSR);

- Any person with respect to whom there are serious reasons for considering that: (a) he has committed a crime against peace, a war crime, or a crime against humanity; (b) he has committed a serious non-political crime outside the country of refuge prior to his admission to that country as a refugee; or (c) he has been guilty of acts contrary to the purposes and principles of the UN (art. 1.F CRSR).

c. Rights of Refugees and Duties of States Parties

The convention goes on to define the rights of individuals who are granted asylum and the responsibilities of nations that grant asylum. The basic principle under the Convention is that refugees should be granted no less favorable treatment than similarly situated foreign residents under the law of their host countries.

States parties to the Convention are obliged to protect refugees that are in their territory and to guarantee their rights to favorable conditions for gainful employment and for the practice of the liberal professions, housing, public education, and access to public relief, among other rights. They may not discriminate as to the admission of refugees on the basis of race, religion, or country of origin.

States parties also must "co-operate with the Office of the United Nations High Commissioner for Refugees, or any other agency of the United Nations which may succeed it, in the exercise of its functions, and shall in particular facilitate its duty of supervising the application of the provisions of [the] Convention" (art. 35 CRSR). States moreover agree to "communicate to the Secretary-General of the United Nations the laws and regulations which they may adopt to ensure the application of [the] Convention" (art. 36 CRSR).

d. Refugees Unlawfully in the Country of Refuge

It is not necessary for individuals claiming refugee status to lawfully enter the state where they make the claim: "The Contracting States shall not impose penalties, on account of their illegal entry or presence, on refugees who, coming directly from a territory where their life or freedom was threatened … enter or are present in their territory without authorization, provided they present themselves without delay to the authorities and show good cause for their illegal entry or presence" (art. 31(1) CRSR).

2. The Contracting States shall not apply to the movements of such refugees restrictions other than those which are necessary and such restrictions shall only be applied until their status in the country is regularized or they obtain admission into another country. The Contracting States shall allow such refugees a reasonable period and all the necessary facilities to obtain admission into another country.

e. Non-Refoulement

While refugees are entitled to the same basic human rights as everyone else, the particular right held by refugees is the right of *non-refoulement*. The principle of *non-refoulement* establishes a refugee's right to be protected against forcible return to territories where his life or freedom would be in danger. This principle places an absolute obligation on states parties not to return refugees to countries in which their lives or freedom would be in danger. The CRSR states that "no Contracting State shall expel or return ("refouler") a refugee in any manner whatsoever to the frontiers of territories where his life or freedom would be threatened on account of his race, religion, nationality, membership of a particular social group or political opinion" (art. 33(1) CRSR). Because the treaty applies in situations where the individual's "life or freedom *would be* threatened" (emphasis added), the standard is an objective one that does not take into account the individual's perception as to whether his life or liberty would be threatened.

In practice, this means that once a refugee arrives at immigration control at an airport or seaport to claim refugee status, he should not be turned away. Nor should he be required to leave while his application is pending, provided he makes a *prima facie* claim.

The principle of *non-refoulement* is widely accepted as a part of customary international law that is binding even on those non-parties to the CRSR. However, there are exceptions to its practice. *Non-refoulement* does not apply when there are "reasonable grounds for regarding as a danger to the security" of the state of refuge, or when the refugee has "been convicted by a final judgement of a particularly serious crime [and] constitutes a danger to the community of that country" (art. 33(2) CRSR). The refugee may also be expelled from the state of refuge "on grounds of national security or public order" (art. 32.1 CRSR). However, the state of refuge may be inhibited by practicing this right if relevant provisions to another treaty to which it is a party apply. For example, under article 3 of the Convention against Torture and Other Cruel, Inhuman or Degrading Treatment (1984), the state may be prevented from returning the person to another state if there are grounds to believe that he would be in danger of torture.

4.   The Refugee Framework

a.   *Durable Solutions*

Once an individual has been granted refugee status, it is the obligation of the international community, through the refugee regime, to identify a durable solution that ends the problems associated with displacement for the refugee and allows people to resume their normal lives in a safe environment. There are three traditional durable solutions available for consideration: voluntary repatriation, local integration and resettlement.

i.   Voluntary Repatriation

While it is not always possible, the solution most often preferred is voluntary repatriation. This solution involves the return of the refugee to the country of origin once the threat to to freedom and safety has been removed. Repatriation must be a voluntary decision by the refugee. It is the responsibility of the international community to provide the refugee with clear and accurate information regarding the situation in their country of origin.

ii. Local Integration

The host nation is under no obligation to absorb the refugee population. However, local integration remains one of the primary durable solutions. Under this solution, refugees are granted the full rights of foreign residents and are assimilated into the local community with access to jobs, education, health care and basic services. If the host nation is unwilling to integrate the refugee into their society, then the third durable solution of resettlement is available.

iii. Resettlement

Resettlement is a means by which several countries can share the responsibility of protecting refugees, rather than placing the entire burden on countries adjacent to refugee-producing situations. There are seventeen countries with resettlement programs: Argentina, Australia, Benin, Brazil, Burkina Faso, Canada, Chile, Denmark, Finland, Iceland, Ireland, Netherlands, New Zealand, Norway, Sweden, the United Kingdom, and the United States. The resettlement programs move refugees from a host nation to a third nation where they are granted permanent residence. Each nation with a resettlement program sets the conditions for resettlement.

b.   *Temporary Settlements for Refugees*

Refugee camps are a significant component of the refugee regime. In the camps, refugees are identified and registered and wait for a "durable solution" to materialize. Humanitarian aid earmarked for refugees is distributed in the camps, which become a means of serving the refugees with educational services, health care, food, water, and temporary shelter, all while maintaining control of the population until a long-term solution is identified.

Many refugees do not like the confinement of the camps and choose to move to the urban centers of the host nation. This presents many challenges, both for refugees and for the refugee administration. Urban refugees tend to move more often, making it difficult for refugee agency caseworkers to keep track of them. They are also vulnerable in urban settings because they may be mistaken by local authorities as illegal immigrants as opposed to refugees with a right to employment. Urban refugees often settle in areas with limited access to education, health services, and low quality housing and may need to address hostility from urban residents who do no distinguish them from growing numbers of unwelcome economic migrants.

c. Partners in the Refugee Administrative System

The last component of the refugee regime includes the national agencies that engage in refugee administration. For many countries, the agency addressing refugee status determination and administration is the same agency that handles immigration, normally within a ministry of foreign affairs. When a country has an immigration office, but no legislation and no procedures to specifically address refugees, the UNHCR will often step in as the primary refugee administration agency. UNHCR's goal is that each nation would have both legislation and institutions for administering refugee protections.

NGOs also play a role in filling the gaps between the UNHCR and national refugee agencies. They may work in refugee camps in the distribution of services, in refugee status determination (RSD), or in advocacy for legislating refugee protections. Together with the national agency for refugee administration, NGOs can participate in a complete or partial parallel administrative system to the system promoted by UNHCR.

5. Regional Conventions

Among the regional conventions that add to or otherwise modify the CRSR are as follow:

- The 1966 Bangkok Principles on Status and Treatment of Refugees adopted at the Asian-African Legal Consultative Committee in 1966;
- The 1969 OAU Convention Governing the Specific Aspects of Refugee Problems in Africa;
- The 1984 Cartagena Declaration on Refugees for Latin America;
- The 1976 Council of Europe's Recommendation 773 on the Situation of de facto Refugees; and
- The 2004 European Union's Council Directive on minimum standards for the qualification and status of third country nationals and stateless persons as refugees or as persons who otherwise need international protection and content of the protection granted.

a. OAU Convention (1969)

The 1969 OAU Convention Governing the Specific Aspects of Refugee Problems in Africa (OAU Refugee Convention) is a regional treaty largely based on the CRSR, but in some respects, expanded its sphere of protection. It adds to the CRSR definition "any person compelled to leave his/her country owing to external aggression, occupation, foreign domination or events seriously disturbing public order in either part or the whole of his country of origin or nationality" (art. 1.2) thus waiving the requirement of genuine persecution due to race, religion, nationality, membership of a particular social group or political opinion.

b. Cartagena Declaration (1984)

The 1984 Cartagena Declaration on Refugees was adopted by several Latin American governments in 1984. Like the OAU Refugee Convention, the Declaration enlarges the CRSR's concept of refugee and includes "persons who have fled their country because their lives, safety or freedom have been threatened by generalized violence, foreign aggression, internal conflicts, massive violation of human rights or other circumstances which have seriously disturbed public order" (§ III.3 CDR). Although the Declaration is not legally binding, most Latin American states apply the expanded definition as a matter of practice, and some have incorporated the definition into their domestic law. The Declaration has been endorsed.

VIII. STATE RESPONSIBILITY AND IMMUNITIES FROM JURISDICTION

A. Sovereign and Diplomatic Immunity

1. Introduction

Sovereign states are as a general rule immune from legal jurisdiction; they cannot be civilly sued or criminally prosecuted. This is based on the old adage, "the king can do no wrong," taken from the common law tradition. However, states may waive part or all of this immunity by consenting to be sued or prosecuted in certain cases. This is normally done through the approval of statutes that recognize causes of action that may be brought in the state's courts to try the sovereign for some alleged wrong attributable to the sovereign.

2. Waivers of Sovereign Immunity

a. *International Courts and Tribunals*

This partial waiver of sovereign immunity can increasingly be found in international law, where states willingly grant international courts or tribunals the right to try them for injuries allegedly attributable to state conduct. For example, the ICJ may try any case under international law to which two states have agreed to confer jurisdiction. Numerous examples of the granting of jurisdiction to foreign courts can be found in regional organizations, such as the Council of Europe, to which acceding states must agree to grant jurisdiction to the ECHR for human rights cases initiated by their nationals or residents.

b. *Domestic Courts*

As discussed in the Remedies section of Chapter 7 – Human Rights and Related Topics (*see supra.*), some nations also allow their residents to bring suit against them in their own domestic courts for civil rights violations, torts, and other wrongs committed by the state or by state actors. Such suits are brought under legislation whereby the state allows itself to be sued under certain circumstances. As mentioned above, this legislation, especially in the common law countries, often allows citizens to sue the state or state actors for civil rights abuses (*e.g.*, discrimination), but it may also extend to ordinary torts or even criminal law.[1]

For example, in the US, federal district courts may under the Federal Torts Claims Act hear "civil actions on claims against the United States, for money damages, accruing on and after January 1, 1945, for injury or loss of property, or personal injury or death caused by the negligent or wrongful act or omission of any employee of the Government while acting within the scope of his office or employment, under circumstances where the United States, if a private person, would be liable to the claimant in accordance with the law of the place where the act or omission occurred" (28 USC § 1346(b)(1)). Similarly, the US allows federal district courts as a venue for "any other civil action or claim against the United States, not exceeding $10,000 in amount, founded either upon the Constitution, or any Act of Congress, or any regulation of an executive department, or upon any express or implied contract with the

---

[1] In the case of criminal law, the ability to sue a state actor often arises not from a waiver of sovereign immunity, but from the fact that a state actor was not acting in an official capacity and thus not as an "arm" of the sovereign; thus, sovereign immunity would not apply to begin with. The actor could be sued as an ordinary citizen.

United States, or for liquidated or unliquidated damages in cases not sounding in tort" (28 USC § 1346(a)(2)). The US district courts may thus be used as venues for some human rights violations (*e.g.*, for a discrimination suit against a federal employer), as well as for actions in tort (*e.g.*, negligence) and breach of an express or implied contract.

One can find similar examples in civil law countries. For example, in Spain, the public administration can be held liable for injuries suffered by Spanish citizens attributable to the state. This principle is known as the *responsabilidad patrimonial de la administración pública.*

3.   Diplomatic Immunities

a.   *Diplomatic Missions: an Overview*

Most countries having diplomatic relations establish permanent diplomatic missions in one another's countries, but some, due mostly to financial constraints, do not. Some states that do not have many mutual interests choose for only one of the nations to establish a presence in the other nation or for the two nations to conduct their diplomatic relations via their missions to an international organization, such as the UN. Whatever the arrangement, diplomatic missions are viewed as arms of the sovereign and the rules discussed above apply to them, albeit with the caveats discussed below.

b.   *Diplomatic Immunity*

There are 183 members of the 1961 Vienna Convention on Diplomatic Relations (VCDR). The treaty has been so widely accepted that it has become a source of international customary law authoritative even for the few remaining non-member states. It grants diplomatic mission staff the privileges and immunities necessary for them to carry out their work.

Diplomats thus have complete immunity from criminal prosecution in their receiving states. However, regarding civil and administrative matters, immunity covers all matters that touch the diplomatic agent. This immunity means that the law of the receiving state cannot be applied to the immune person for as long as the immunity lasts and is not waived by the sending state (because the immunity derives from the sovereignty of the state, diplomats cannot waive immunity on their own behalf). The immunity only lasts as long as the individual remains a diplomat. Thereafter, he may be prosecuted by the receiving state for crimes committed within its territory.

Diplomatic immunity does not mean that the immune person is exempt from the laws of his own state. If a serious crime is committed by the immune person, the sending state may recall the immune person back to the sending state to be prosecuted back home. In addition, it may waive his immunity and allow for him to be prosecuted by the receiving state (art. 32 VCLT).

In any event, even with the diplomatic privileges in place, the host nation may "at any time and without having to explain its decision, notify the sending State that the head of the mission or any member of the diplomatic staff of the mission is *persona non grata* or that any other member of the staff of the mission is not acceptable" (art. 9 VCLT). Under such circumstances, the sending state must either recall the person concerned or terminate his functions with the mission.

c.   *Other Diplomatic Protections and Guarantees*

In addition to these provisions, the Vienna Convention holds the premises of a diplomatic mission (*e.g.*, the embassy) to be inviolate; the host country may only enter with the permission of the head of the mission (art. 22 VCDR), and it provides for the "free communication between the diplomats of the mission and their home country" and protections of the diplomatic bag (art. 27 VCDR).

B. State Responsibility

1. Generally

a. Overview

The laws of state responsibility govern when and how a state is held responsible for a breach of its international obligations. They determine when an obligation has been breached and the legal consequences of that violation. In this way they are "secondary" rules that address basic issues of responsibility and remedies available for breach of "primary" or substantive rules of international law. For example, the rules relating to the use of armed force are primary rules of international law; the rules determining whether a state breached these rules—the laws of state responsibility—are secondary rules that provide a framework to define injury, claims, and remedies. The rules governing state responsibility establish: (i) the conditions for an act to qualify as internationally wrongful; (ii) the circumstances under which actions of officials, private individuals and other entities may be attributed to the state; (iii) general defenses to liability; and (iv) the consequences of liability.

The Draft Articles on the Responsibility of States for Internationally Wrongful Acts (DARS), colloquially known as the "Draft Articles on State Responsibility," was adopted by the ILC in 2001 as an attempt to summarize and codify the customary international legal rules for state responsibility. It is a non-binding declaration that serves as evidence of customary international law. The Articles are divided into three parts:

b. Definition and Elements

i. Overview

Under the Draft Articles, "every internationally wrongful act of a State entails the international responsibility of that State" (art. 1 DARS). By "wrongful act," DARS signals not only acts, but also omissions (*see, e.g.*, art. 2). An act *or omission* of a state is an internationally wrongful act when it "(a) Is attributable to the State under international law; and (b) Constitutes a breach of an international obligation of the State" (art. 2 DARS). Such breaches of international obligations may include the breach of a treaty or the violation of another state's territory.

ii. Attributable Conduct

Breaches of international obligations are attributable to a state when the state acts through people with a mantle of authority exercising the state's power. Such breaches may also include injurious acts committed by a state's *internal organ* or by a *person* or *entity* exercising governmental authority, even if such a person or entity "exceeds its authority or contravenes instructions," so long as it was acting in an official capacity (art. 7 DARS). Injurious acts are also considered breaches of states' international obligations when committed by persons acting under the instructions, direction, or control of the state (art. 8 DARS).

A state is further responsible for conduct not attributable to a state if and to the extent that the state later "*acknowledges* and *adopts* the conduct in question as its own" (art. 11 DARS). This was the case of the Iran Hostages Case, in which students took over the American embassy in Iran and the new Islamic government of Iran ratified the takeover after it occurred. In the United States Diplomatic and Consular Staff in Tehran case (*United States of America v. Iran* (1982)), the ICJ held that although the Islamic government did not have any connection to the takeover, the conduct could be attributed to the government because of the government's ratification thereof. The Court held that "the militants, authors of the invasion and jailers of the hostages, had now become agents of the Iranian State for whose acts the State itself was internationally responsible."

A state act or omission is not, however, internationally wrongful if conducted with another state's consent (art. 20 DARS), if it "constitutes a lawful measure of self-defence taken in conformity with the Charter of the United Nations" (art. 21 DARS), is a permitted countermeasure taken by a state injured by the wrongful act of another state in order to pressure the other state into compliance with its obligations (art. 22 DARS), resulted from *force majeure* (art. 23 DARS), a situation of distress requiring the act in order to save lives (art. 24 DARS), or a situation of necessity whereby the act is required to safeguard an "essential interest" of the state and no essential interest of a third state is impaired (art. 25 DARS). None of these exceptions are to imply that a state is excused from the wrongfulness of an act that contravenes peremptory norms of general international law (art. 26 DARS).

States are further not responsible for conduct of a non-state character, such as acts or omissions of private persons, criminals, or terrorist networks, if such conduct is not supported or endorsed by the state. In a similar vein, a state is not responsible for the acts of unsuccessful insurgents who retain non-state status. However, if insurgents are successful, they attain state status and become responsible for actions undertaken during their insurgency.

c. Preconditions to Legal Adjudication

Two preconditions must be met before suit can be brought against a state for injury to a non-citizen under international law—(i) *bond of nationality*; and (ii) *exhaustion of remedies*— in accordance with the following framework:

- *Bond of nationality.* The claim is not brought in accordance with applicable rules relating to the nationality of claims (art. 44(a) DARS). A state bringing suit against another state for injury to its nationals must show that those harmed are nationals with *bona fide* links to the state under the applicable provisions of international law.

- *Exhaustion of local remedies.* The claim is one to which the rule of exhaustion of local remedies applies and any available and effective local remedy has not been exhausted (art. 44(b) DARS). If the injury is one over which the injuring state's courts have local jurisdiction, then before claiming state responsibility, the injured party or parties must bring suit and exhaust any other applicable local remedies, unless doing so can be shown to be ineffective. For example, before a state could raise a claim against the US for state responsibility, the injured parties would need to first adjudicate the claim under the US Alien Tort Claims Act, which grants US federal courts jurisdiction to hear claims by aliens.

State responsibility claims are thus inadmissible when a state has failed to show that those harmed are its nationals or when local remedies were not exhausted.

d. Reparation

Full reparation in the form of "restitution, compensation and satisfaction, either singly or in combination" are required of a state for an injury caused by its internationally wrongful act (art. 34 DARS). Restitution refers to the restoration of the situation existing before the wrongful act was committed (art. 35 DARS). When this is not possible or is unreasonably burdensome, the state must make compensation for the damage (art. 36 DAR) or, when this is not possible, satisfaction for the injury. Satisfaction may take the form of "an acknowledgement of the breach, an expression of regret, [or] a formal apology" (art. 37 DARS).

e. International Crimes

Traditionally, individuals have been held responsible for international crimes such as torture, genocide, and aggression. This has been the policy of international criminal tribunals beginning with the Nuremberg IMT and the IMTFE, and more recently, the ICTY, ICTR, and SLSC, all of which tried individuals, not states, for international crimes. The ICC follows this approach.

There was thus a great outcry when the ILC, in its 1996 draft on State Responsibility, suggested that states can be held responsible for international crimes. In addition to how such acts could attach to a state and not to individual actors, a series of questions relating to the definitions of such crimes arose.

The 2001 DARS left out this divisive question, but includes a chapter in Part Two on "Serious breaches of obligations under peremptory norms of general international law." When such breaches are committed, all states are under an obligation to "cooperate to bring to an end through lawful means" any such breaches (art. 41 DARS). Presumably, this would include states' rights to invoke universal jurisdiction in trying the actors involved.

f. Implementation

When invoking a state's responsibility, the injured state must give notice of its claim to the injuring state. The injured state may indicate what form reparation should take in repairing the injury (art. 43 DARS). In the event the injuring state fails to make sure reparations, the injured state may take countermeasures comprised of "the non-performance for the time being of international obligations of the State" against the injuring state in order to induce it to comply with its obligations (art. 49 DARS).

2. Injury to Aliens

a. Overview

Traditionally, when an alien was injured by another state, because the claim belonged to the state of the alien's citizenship, the state of the alien's citizenship brought the claim on behalf of the alien against the injuring state. If reparations were paid to the state of the victim's nationality, that state was not required to pay the individual, since it was the state's claim.

Today, however, individual aliens may file claims against states for injuries attributable to the states when certain elements are met. Such claims fall under the regime of state responsibility to aliens. This legal regime is distinct from the general regime of state responsibility: while the law of state responsibility is a framework that provides a structure to define injury, claims, and remedies, state responsibility for injury to aliens is a substantive part of international law that has its own laws. Thus, whereas the general regime of state responsibility is comprised of secondary laws, the regime of state responsibility to aliens is comprised of primary (substantive) norms.

b. Standard of Treatment Applied to Foreign Nationals

Regarding the standard of treatment that should be applied to foreign nationals, two views are available: the objective view and the equality of treatment view.

i. Objective View

Under the majority objective view, states should adhere to an objective minimum standard that gives rise to responsibility for human rights violations, personal rights violations, and property rights or economic interest violations that requires states to protect noncitizens to the best of their ability.

ii. Equality of Treatment View

Developing countries simply may lack the resources to carry out this minimum standard of treatment. This is why, in many Latin American countries, the minority equality of treatment view is held: a state fulfills its duty towards foreign nationals when it gives it the same treatment as it does to its own citizens. should be sufficient. This is because many Latin American countries have a low standard of treatment for their own citizens and do not wish to have to apply a higher standard to noncitizens.

c. Elements

As discussed above, state responsibility lies for injuries attributable to a state's act or omission when it is (i) attributable to the state; and (ii) in violation of the state's international obligations (art. 2 DARS). This same rule, which applies under many states' national legislations for injuries caused to their own citizens, applies as a principle under international law to wrongful acts by states to aliens within their territories. The legal regime outlined above regarding what constitutes state attribution also applies herein.

d. Property Rights of Foreign Nationals: State Expropriation

Under the Restatement of the Foreign Relations Law, state expropriation of land historically assigned responsibility to a state if it takes property of a national of another state that (i) is not for a public purpose; or (ii) is discriminatory; or (iii) is not justly compensated. Compensation is just if it is an amount equivalent to the value of the property and is paid at the time of the taking or within a reasonable time thereafter (RFR § 712).

UN General Assembly Resolution 1803 (1962) and the Charter of Economic Rights and Duties of States (1974) are both statutes concerning takings. The GA resolution follows traditional takings law by saying that states must follow existing international law when taking property and that "just" compensation "must" be paid to the person from whom the land is taken. The Charter of Economic Rights and Duties of States requires compensation controversies to be settled using the "domestic law of the nationalizing State and by its tribunals"—not by international law—and holds that "appropriate" compensation "should" be paid to the person from whom the land is taken. The preference of the US is the GA resolution.

IX. INTERNATIONAL ENVIRONMENTAL LAW AND RELATED TOPICS

A. Introduction

International environmental law operates to regulate the interaction of humanity with the environment. It seeks to reduce the impact of human activity on the natural environment. Environmental law draws from and is influenced by principles of environmentalism, including ecology, conservation, stewardship, responsibility and sustainability.

From an economic perspective, environmental laws may be understood as concerned with the preservation of resources from exhaustion.

B. Guiding Principles

Some of the guiding principles governing the development and administration of international environmental law include:

- *Duty to Warn.* There is a duty to promptly warn other states of environmental damages to which they may be exposed;
- *Principle of good neighborliness.* This is set out, for example, in Principle 21 of the Stockholm Declaration;
- *Polluter pays principle.* Basis for resolving transboundary environmental disputes established in the *Trail Smelter Arbitration* (1941);
- *The precautionary principle.* If an action has a suspected risk of causing harm to the environment, in the absence of scientific consensus that the action is harmful, the burden of proof that it is not harmful falls on those acting;
- *The principle of sustainable development.* Development must be planned and administered in ways that are sustainable; and
- *Environmental procedural rights.* Rules should be instituted granting civil society access to justice, information, and participation (see Principle 10 of the 1992 Rio Declaration).

C. World Summits and Treaties

The issues governed by environment law, including pollution control, global warming, the dangers of nuclear substances, and resource conservation, are global in nature and reach across borders. They cannot be effectively tackled without international cooperation. Recognizing the common interest of all nations to establish policies for sustainable development, the international community has come together to

1. United Nations Conference on the Human Environment (1972)

The United Nations Conference on the Human Environment, informally known as the "Stockholm Conference," was a UN conference convened in Stockholm in 1972 and attended by representatives of 113 countries, 19 inter-governmental agencies, and more than 400 inter-governmental and non-governmental organizations. In addition to founding UNEP to oversee UN environmental programs, the Conference produced the following documents:

- *Declaration of the United Nations Conference on the Human Environment*, informally known as the "Stockholm Declaration," contains 26 principles concerning the human environment and development. It seeks to preserve and enhance the environment and enjoin states from causing environmental damage to other states or areas beyond their jurisdiction;

- *Action Plan*, containing 109 recommendations; and

- *Resolution Convening of a Second United Nations Conference on the Human Environment*, recommending the GA to convene a second UN Conference on the Human Environment.

2. World Commission on Environment and Development (1983)

The World Commission on Environment and Development (WCED), informally known as the "Brundtland Commission," was convened by the UN in 1983 to address concerns about the deterioration of the human environment and natural resources and its consequences on economic and social development. The Commission was established by UN GA Resolution 38/161 in 1983. The Commission published a report, *Our Common Future*, which searches for international multilateralism and interdependence in the search for sustainable development.

3. Vienna Conference on Ozone Layer Depletion (1985)

The Vienna Conference on ozone layer depletion was convened in Vienna in 1985 when a hole in the ozone layer in the South Pole was detected. The international community drafted and adopted the Vienna Convention for the Protection of the Ozone Layer (1985), which entered into force in 1988 as a framework for the international efforts to protect the ozone layer.

The Convention does not include legally binding reduction goals for the use of chlorofluorocarbons (CFCs), the main ozone-depleting chemical agents; these are laid out in the accompanying Montreal Protocol on Substances that Deplete the Ozone Layer, informally known as the "Montreal Protocol," which was opened for signature in 1987 and entered into force in 1989. There are currently 196 states parties.

4. United Nations Conference on Environment and Development (1992)

a. Overview

The United Nations Conference on Environment and Development (UNCED) (1992), better known as the "Earth Summit" or "Earth Summit 1992," was an international environmental summit attended by representatives of 172 governments, including 108 heads of state or government, and 2,400 representatives of NGOs, and 17,000 people at the parallel NGO "Global Forum," with Consultative Status. The Earth Summit addressed systematic scrutiny of patterns of production, especially of toxic or poisonous materials; alternative sources of energy to replace the use of fossil fuels linked to climate change; new reliance on public transportation systems in order to reduce vehicle emissions, pollution, and congestion in cities; and water scarcity.

b. Resulting Treaties and Declarations

The Earth Summit resulted in the following treaties and protocols:

- *The Convention on Biological Diversity*. Informally known as the "Biodiversity Convention," this binding treaty was opened for signature at the Earth Summit in 1992 and entered into force in 1993. It made a start towards redefinition of money supply measures that did not inherently encourage destruction of natural ecoregions and so-called uneconomic growth;

- *UN Framework Convention on Climate Change (UNFCCC)*. Also known as the "Climate Change Convention," this binding convention was adopted in 1992 and entered into force in 1994 with 192 parties. It seeks to stabilize greenhouse gas concentrations in the atmosphere at a level that would prevent interference with the climate system. The Convention is best known for leading to the Kyoto Protocol, adopted in 1997 (entering into force 2005) to limit greenhouse gas emissions. It currently has 191 states parties (the US signed but did not ratify the Protocol; Afghanistan, Andorra, and Vatican City have neither signed nor ratified it). The UNFCCC together with the Kyoto Protocol build on the efforts of the Montreal Protocol in limiting the emission of greenhouse gases.

- *Agreement not to "carry out any activities on the lands of indigenous peoples that would cause environmental degradation or that would be culturally inappropriate."*

The Earth Summit also produced the following non-binding documents:

- *Rio Declaration on Environment and Development*. Informally known as the "Rio Declaration," it established 27 principles intended to guide sustainable development around the world.

- *Agenda 21*. A UN action plan that outlines strategies for cleaning up the environment and encouraging environmentally sound development. Work on the text began in 1989 and 178 governments voted to adopt the program at the Earth Summit.

- *Statement of Principles on Forests*. Formally known as the "Non-Legally Binding Authoritative Statement of Principles for a Global Consensus on the Management, Conservation and Sustainable Development of All Types of Forests," and informally as the "Forest Principles," it was produced at the Earth Summit to preserve the world's tropical rainforests and recommends that nations monitor the impact of development on their forests and limit the damage done to them.

The Green Cross International was founded at the Earth Summit to follow up on the Summit's work.

5. World Summit on Sustainable Development (2002)

Informally known as "Earth Summit 2002" or "Rio + 10," the World Summit on Sustainable Development (WSSD) was convened in Johannesburg to discuss sustainable development by the United Nations. The Summit gathered a number of leaders from business and non-governmental organizations and led to the following agreements:

- Johannesburg Declaration;
- *Johannesburg Plan of Implementation*, as an action plan;

- Johannesburg, 27 August: agreement was made to restore the world's depleted fisheries for 2015.

D. UN Environmental Programme

The United Nations Environment Programme (UNEP), headquartered in Nairobi, was founded in 1972 at the UN Conference on the Human Environment to coordinate the development of environmental policy consensus by keeping the global environment under review and bringing emerging issues to the attention of governments and the international community for action. It is governed by UN GA resolution 2997 (XXVII) (1972) and subsequent amendments adopted at UNCED in 1992; the Nairobi Declaration on the Role and Mandate of UNEP; and the Malmö Ministerial Declaration of 31 May 2000. UNEP has played a significant role in developing international environmental conventions, promoting environmental science and information, working on the development and implementation of policy with national governments and regional institution, working in conjunction with environmental NGOs, and funding and implementing environmentally related development projects.

E. Nuclear Non-Proliferation

Among the international legal instruments governing *nuclear non-proliferation* are as follow:

- *The Treaty Banning Nuclear Weapon Tests in the Atmosphere, in Outer Space and Under Water ("Nuclear Test Ban Treaty")* (1963). Prohibits all test detonations of nuclear weapons except underground. It was signed in August 1963 and entered into force in September 1963. Most countries are states parties; China, France, North Korea, and Saudi Arabia are among states that have not.
- *Non-Proliferation Treaty* (1968). A treaty that aims to control the spread of nuclear weapons. The treaty has been signed by over 175 nations.
- *Comprehensive Nuclear Test Ban Treaty* (1996). A proposed treaty to prohibit all testing of nuclear weapons in all environments, including underground, underwater, in the atmosphere, on land, and in space. It currently has 182 signatories and 153 ratifications. It will enter force when 44 states enumerated in Annex 2 ratify the treaty. At present, 35 Annex 2 states have ratified the treaty, and the following 9 have not: China, Egypt, Indonesia, India, Iran, Israel, North Korea, Pakistan, and the United States (the U.S. Senate in 1999 refused to ratify the treaty).

X. THE LAW OF THE SEA, AIR, AND SPACE

A. Law of the Sea

1. Overview

The law of the sea deals principally with issues involving the exploitation, ownership, and use of the sea as both a means of communication and as a reservoir of resources. The law has developed gradually through customs embedded in state practices over the centuries, and the twentieth century saw the codification of much of this custom in the law of the sea conventions of 1958 and 1982. These deal with the competing rights and responsibilities of coastal states and foreign states with respect to territorial and contiguous seas, exclusive economic zones, continental shelves, and the high seas.

2. Legal Instruments

a. Four Conventions of the Law of the Sea of 1958

In 1956, the UN held its first Conference on the Law of the Sea (UNCLOS I) in Geneva. UNCLOS I resulted in four treaties concluded in 1958:

- *Convention on the Territorial Sea and Contiguous Zone (GCTS)*. It confirmed coastal states' right to claim a territorial sea, over which their sovereignty extends, and sets out the principles by which the limits of the territorial sea may be determined. However, it did not specify the breadth of the territorial sea. The Convention also established the concept of the contiguous zone, in which the coastal state enjoys limited jurisdiction for enforcing customs, fiscal, sanitary, and immigration laws.
- *Convention on the Continental Shelf*. It incorporated then existing rules and created new rules;
- *Convention on the High Seas*. Unlike the other three 1958 Geneva Conventions, which created new rules, it generally declares "established principles of international law" (Preamble); and
- *Convention on Fishing and Conservation of Living Resources of the High Seas*. It incorporated then existing rules and created new rules.

b. United Nations Convention on the Law of the Sea (1982)

Whereas the second Conference on the Law of the Sea ("UNCLOS II") of 1960 failed to produce any new agreements, the third United Nations Conference on the Law of the Sea ("UNCLOS III"), which took place from 1974 through 1982, resulted in the United Nations Convention on the Law of the Sea (UNCLOS), colloquially known as the "Law of the Sea Convention." UNCLOS was concluded and signed in 1982 and entered into force in 1994, a year after Guyana became the 60th state to sign the treaty. With 320 articles and 9 annexes, the Convention defines the rights and responsibilities of nations in their use of the world's oceans and establishes guidelines for businesses and the management of marine natural resources. It formed an international framework for law over all ocean space, its uses and resources, and established the International Tribunal for the Law of the Sea (ITLS) and the

International Seabed Authority. At present, 158 countries and the European Community have joined the Convention.

3. Maritime Zones of Jurisdiction

The following provisions apply to the various maritime zones that coastal states hold jurisdiction over. Determinations of the breadth and locations of the internal and territorial waters, contiguous zones, exclusive economic zones, and continental shelves explained herein apply not only to coasts of coastal states, but to their islands as well.

a. Internal Waters

Internal waters are the inland lakes, rivers, and ports located within the boundaries of a state. They are classified as appertaining to the land territory of the coastal state. There is no right of innocent passage of other states.

Ships of foreign states are under the jurisdiction of the coastal state when in the state's internal waters. The coastal state is sovereign over these waters and is fully entitled to enforce its laws against foreign marine ships. It has jurisdiction over the ship and events occurring thereon. However, if the ship is a warship, it is immune from enforcement without the authorization of the captain or of the flag state, as military vessels are viewed as arms of the sovereignty of the flag state. However, the coastal state may require such vessels to leave immediately.

b. Territorial Sea

i. Breadth and Methods for Drawing Baselines

The territorial sea is located not more than "12 nautical miles, measured from baselines" determined in accordance with UNCLOS (art. (art. 3 UNCLOS). The baseline is usually the low-water mark—the location of the coastline at low tide.

There are three methods for drawing baselines:

- *Normal method.* The normal baseline for measuring the width of the territorial sea is the "low-water line along the coast as marked on large-scale charts officially recognized by the coastal State" (art. 5 UNCLOS).

- *Reefs.* "In the case of islands situated on atolls or of islands having fringing reefs, the baseline for measuring the breadth of the territorial sea is the seaward low-water line of the reef, as shown by the appropriate symbol on charts officially recognized by the coastal State" (art. 6 UNCLOS).

- *Straight baselines.* When the coastline is deeply indented and cut into or has a fringe islands in its immediate vicinity (*e.g.,* the case of Chile), straight baselines joining appropriate points may be used (art. 7.1 UNCLOS).

When a coast is marked by a bay, it is accepted practice that a straight baseline from which to determine the breadth of the territorial sea may be drawn across the mouth of the bay. However, under UNCLOS, "If the distance between the low-water marks of the natural entrance points of a bay does not exceed 24 nautical miles, a closing line may be drawn between these two low-water marks, and the waters enclosed thereby shall be considered as internal waters" (art. 10.4 UNCLOS). Otherwise, a straight baseline of 24 miles may be drawn "within the bay in such a manner as to enclose the maximum area of water that is possible with a line of that length" (art. 10.5 UNCLOS). However, this provision does not apply to so-called "historic bays" (bays whose waters are treated by the coastal state as internal in light of historic rights and general acquiescence) or in cases in which straight baselines are applies (art. 10.6 UNCLOS).

Where the coasts of two states are opposite or adjacent to each other, neither of the two states is entitled (absent agreement to the contrary or historic or special circumstances) "to extend its territorial sea beyond the median line every point of which is equidistant from the nearest points on the baselines from which the breadth of the territorial seas of each of the two States is measured" (art. 15 UNCLOS).

ii. Rights of States and Innocent Passage

States have full sovereignty over their territorial seas. They possess the exclusive right to fish in their territorial seas, exploit their seabed resources, and regulate the airspace above (cabotage). Certain powers of arrest over merchant ships exist in the territorial seas, with the exception of international straits, such as the Strait of Hormuz, linking the Gulf of Oman and the Persian Gulf, or the English Channel, which hold more favorable rules towards foreign ships.

Foreign merchant vessels have the right to innocent passage in the coastal state's territorial waters. Passage is innocent "so long as it is not prejudicial to the peace, good order or security of the coastal State" (art. 19.1 UNCLOS). As a basic principle, the foreign ship, in order to enjoy the right of innocent passage while in the coastal state's territorial waters, may not engage in any activity not having a direct bearing on passage. UNCLOS specifically enumerates the following activities, all of which are considered prejudicial to the coastal state, as prohibited: any threat or use of force against the sovereignty, territorial integrity or political independence of the coastal state; any exercise or practice with weapons; any act aimed at collecting information to the prejudice of the defense or security of the coastal state; any act of propaganda aimed at affecting the defense or security of the coastal state; the launching, landing or taking on board of any aircraft or military device; the loading or unloading of any commodity, currency or person contrary to the laws and regulations of the coastal state; acts of willful and serious pollution; fishing; research or survey activities; acts aimed at interfering with systems of communication of the coastal state (art. 19.2 UNCLOS). Western powers hold that the right to innocent passage extends to warships, but third world countries disagree.

Coastal states may exercise criminal jurisdiction to arrest any person or to conduct any investigation in connection with any crime committed on board a foreign ship passing through its territorial sea, but article 27.1 UNCLOS limits this right to the following cases only:

> (a) if the consequences of the crime extend to the coastal State;
> (b) if the crime is of a kind to disturb the peace of the country or the good order of the territorial sea;
> (c) if the assistance of the local authorities has been requested by the master of the ship or by a diplomatic agent or consular officer of the flag State; or
> (d) if such measures are necessary for the suppression of illicit traffic in narcotic drugs or psychotropic substances.

The coastal state should not stop or divert the passing ship in order to exercise civil jurisdiction in relation to a person on board the ship (art. 28 UNCLOS).

c. Contiguous Zone

The contiguous zone is a zone contiguous to a coastal state's territorial sea. Article 33.1 UNCLOS permits the coastal state to exercise the control necessary to:

> (a) prevent infringement of its customs, fiscal, immigration or sanitary laws and regulations within its territory or territorial sea;
>
> (b) punish infringement of the above laws and regulations committed within its territory or territorial sea.

The contiguous zone may extend up to 24 nautical miles from the baselines from which the breadth of the territorial sea is measured (art 33.2 UNCLOS). Whereas under the 1958 GCTS, this zone formed a part of the high seas, at present it forms part of the exclusive economic zone.

d. Exclusive Economic Zone

The exclusive economic zone is located up to 200 nautical miles from the baselines used to measure the territorial waters (art. 57 UNCLOS). The exclusive economic zone grants the coastal state sovereign rights for the purpose of exploring and exploiting, conserving and managing both the living and non-living natural resources of the waters superjacent to the seabed and of the seabed and its subsoil, and with regard to other activities for the economic exploitation and exploration of the zone, such as the production of energy from the water, currents and winds (art. 56.1(a) UNCLOS). The exclusive economic zone also entitles the coastal state to jurisdiction with regard to: "(i) the establishment and use of artificial islands, installations and structures; (ii) marine scientific research; (iii) the protection and preservation of the marine environment; (c) other rights and duties provided for in this Convention" (art. 56.1(b) UNCLOS).

e. Continental Shelf Zone

i. Definition and Limits

In geology, the continental shelf refers to the ledge that projects from the continental landmass into the deep sea, connecting one to the other. Compared to the deep sea, which reaches thousands of meters of depth, the continental shelf, before falling away into the deep sea, is relatively shallow, usually at less than 200 meters deep. In terms of how far it projects from the coast, the figures vary widely. While in some coastal states, the continental shelf may be within the territorial waters, in others, it may protrude many hundreds of miles from coast. For example, in Chile, the continental shelf is within the territorial sea, and in California, it is only 5 miles from the coastline. In contrast, the entire North Sea is situated above a continental shelf.

Because of the rich natural resources, including oil and gas, and fishing available in the continental shelf zones, the rights to continental shelves have been highly sought after by states and have thus fallen under the regulations of the law of the sea conventions. Under UNCLOS, the continental shelf of a coastal state is defined as "the seabed and subsoil of the submarine areas that extend beyond its territorial sea throughout the natural prolongation of its land territory to the outer edge of the continental margin" (art. 76.1 UNCLOS). If the outer edge of the continental margin does not extend beyond 200 nautical miles from the baselines from which the territorial sea is measured (as in the case of Chile and the west coast of the

US), then the shelf will automatically be considered under UNCLOS to be located at 200 nautical miles from the baselines (art. 76.1 UNCLOS). Otherwise, its location is determined by its natural geological formation. However, even in this latter case, the outer limits of the continental shelf may not extend beyond 350 nautical miles from the baselines used to measure the territorial sea or 100 nautical miles from the 2,500 metre isobath (a line connecting the depth of 2,500 metres) (art. 76.5 UNCLOS).

ii. Rights of the Coastal State

The coastal state exercises over the continental shelf sovereign rights for the purpose of exploring it and exploiting its natural resources, defined as the mineral and other non-living resources of the seabed and subsoil and living *sedentary* organisms (organisms which, at the harvestable stage, either are immobile on or under the seabed or are unable to move except in constant physical contact with the seabed or the subsoil). This right is exclusive in the sense that no one may undertake these activities without the express consent of the coastal state (art. 77 UNCLOS). However, the rights of the coastal state over the continental shelf "do not affect the legal status of the superjacent waters or of the air space above those waters" (art. 78.1 UNCLOS).

f. High Seas

i. Definition

The high seas are defined under UNCLOS as "all parts of the sea that are not included in the exclusive economic zone, in the territorial sea or in the internal waters of a State, or in the archipelagic waters of an archipelagic State" (art. 86 UNCLOS). The high seas is located beyond the continental shelf boundary, over the deep seabed.

ii. Freedoms

As a general rule, the high seas are open, and with the exception of the doctrines of recognition, acquiescence, and prescription, no state "may validly purport to subject any part of the high seas to its sovereignty" (art. 89 UNCLOS). Freedom of the high seas comprises, subject to limitations, freedom of navigation; freedom of overflight; freedom to lay submarine cables and pipelines; freedom to construct artificial islands and other installations; freedom of fishing; and freedom of scientific research (art. 87.1 UNCLOS). However, the high seas may only be used for peaceful purposes (art. 88 UNCLOS); nuclear testing or military exercises are prohibited.

As a general rule, under the principle of freedom of navigation in the high seas, coastal states may not stop foreign flagged vessels. However, in the case of hot pursuit, if the coastal state has been pursuing a vessel and the pursuit commenced in the coastal state's internal or archipelagic waters, territorial sea, or contiguous zone, it may pursue the vessel even if it crosses into the high seas if the pursuit has not been interrupted (art. 111.1 UNCLOS). This right ceases "as soon as the ship pursued enters the territorial sea of its own State or of a third State" (art. 111.3 UNCLOS).

4. Jurisdiction and Enforcement of Law

In the high seas, ships are subject to international law and to the law of the state whose flag they are carrying (the "flag state"), which corresponds to the nationality of the ship.

There must be a "genuine link" between the ship and the flag state (art. 91 UNCLOS), which enforces both international law and its own law.

5. Legal Institutions

a. International Tribunal for the Law of the Sea

The International Tribunal for the Law of the Sea (ITLS) is an intergovernmental organization created by the mandate of the Third United Nations Conference on the Law of the Sea (UNCLOS III) and established by UNCLOS. The ITLS has authority to settle disputes between its 155 member states.

b. International Seabed Authority

The International Seabed Authority (ISA) is an independent treaty body created by UNCLOS to organize and control all mineral-related activities in the international seabed area beyond the limits of national jurisdiction. It issues licenses to states to exploit the resources of the deep seabed beyond the limits of national jurisdiction and is responsible for the regulation of seabed mining. Based in Kingston, Jamaica, the ISA is funded by a tax issued on continental shelf exploration

B. Air Law

1. Regulatory Framework

Air law, also known as "aviation law," conventionally refers to that body of laws concerning civil aviation. It is sometimes broadly also used to refer to any law involving the use of the air (*e.g.*, those governing radio transmissions), but in this text, only the conventional definition will be used.

Because of the international character of aviation, a large part of air law is comprised of international conventions. One of the earliest legal instruments to this effect was the Convention Relating to the Regulation of Aerial Navigation, colloquially known as the "Paris Convention," which was signed by 27 states in 1919 to deal with a host of aerial issues including certificates of airworthiness of aircraft, the certification and licensing of pilots, admission to air navigation above foreign territories, and departure and landing rules. The Paris Convention recognizes the exclusive sovereignty of each state over airspace above its territory, without prejudice to innocent passage by foreign aircraft. Moreover, it extends to aircraft the principle of nationality, whereby each aircraft must be registered with a state.

Today's basic framework for aviation law is established by the Chicago Convention on International Civil Aviation, commonly referred to as the "Chicago Convention" (CC). The Convention has undergone 8 revisions since its 1947 entry into force. The most recent took place in 2006. The treaty was signed in 1944 by 52 states at Chicago's International Civil Aviation Conference, which also led to the adoption of the International Air Services Transit Agreement, where freedom to fly across the territory of a state without landing and freedom to land for non-traffic purposes was established. As for the Chicago Convention, the principle of the "complete and exclusive sovereignty" of each state over airspace above its territory is reaffirmed (art. 1 CC) and various rules of airspace, aircraft registration, pilot licensing, radio navigation aids, and safety, are set forth. Today, the Convention counts 188 states parties.

The Convention also established the International Civil Aviation Organization (ICAO), a specialized agency that seeks to promote security through cooperative aviation regulation. In

October of 1947, within 6 months of its birth, ICAO became a specialized ECOSOC agency. It is mandated with the planning and development of international air navigation and regulation.

2. Air Carrier Liability

Under the 1929 Warsaw Convention for the Unification of Certain Rules Relating to International Carriage by Air, informally known as the "Warsaw Convention," the owner or operator of a carrier was made liable for any injury, death, or property damage by the carrier.

The Convention for the Unification of Certain Rules for International Carriage, colloquially known as the "Montreal Convention," was adopted in 1999 by a Diplomatic meeting of the member states of the International Civil Aviation Organization to amend important provisions of the 1929 Warsaw Convention's regime concerning compensation for the victims of air disasters. The Convention protects passengers by introducing a two-tier liability system and by facilitating the swift recovery of proven damages without the need for litigation. Air carriers under the Convention are strictly liable for proven damages up to 100,000 Special Drawing Rights (SDRs) (an IMF reserve currency equivalent) or $138,000 per passenger at the time of its ratification by the United States in 2003. Where damages of more than 100,000 SDR are sought, the airline may avoid liability by proving that the accident which caused the injury or death was not due to its negligence. The Convention also amended the jurisdictional provisions of Warsaw and now allows victims or their families to sue foreign carriers where they maintain their principal residence, and requires all air carriers to carry liability insurance.

The Montreal Convention also generally increases the maximum liability of airlines for lost baggage. Whereas liability in the Warsaw Convention is based on the weight of the baggage, the Montreal Convention changes liability to a fixed amount 1000 SDR.

C. Space Law

Outer space lies beyond the upper limit of a state's sovereign airspace. In a 1963 resolution, the UN GA declared outer space to be free for exploration and use by all states. The resolution outlined rules assigning individual responsibility for dealing with transgressions of international law declared space to be incapable of national appropriation.

The basic legal framework of international space law was established with the Treaty on Principles Governing the Activities of States in the Exploration and Use of Outer Space, Including the Moon and Other Celestial Bodies, colloquially known as the "Outer Space Treaty of 1967." Reiterating the principle that the "exploration and use of outer space, including the moon and other celestial bodies, shall be carried out for the benefit and in the interests of all countries" (art. I OST), it bars states parties from placing in orbit around the earth "any objects carrying nuclear weapons or any other kinds of weapons of mass destruction, [installing] such weapons on celestial bodies, or [stationing] such weapons in outer space in any other manner" and reserves the moon and other celestial bodies for exclusively peaceful purposes (art. IV OST). The treaty also sets out a framework of mutual assistance for the rescue of astronauts in crisis situations (art. V OST) and cooperation in the exploration of outer space (art. IX OST).

The Agreement Governing the Activities of States on the Moon and Other Celestial Bodies (1979), informally known as the Moon Treaty (MT), follows the tradition of reserving the regions of outer space to peaceful purposes. It seeks to promote cooperation "in the exploration and use of the moon and other celestial bodies [and] prevent the moon from becoming an area of international conflict" (Preamble MT). It requires the demilitarization of the moon and other celestial bodies and declares that "the moon and its natural resources are the common heritage of mankind" (art. 11.1 MT). However, the effect of the treaty has been minimal, as none of the states engaged in manned space exploration ratified the treaty.

XI. INTERNATIONAL ECONOMIC AND TRADE LAW

Organizations such as the WTO that write international laws binding on member states fall within public international law, as they do not deal with states' domestic laws strictly speaking.

A. Instruments and Institutions

1. General Agreement on Tariffs and Trade

The General Agreement on Tariffs and Trade (GATT) was formed in 1949 and lasted until 1993, when it was replaced by the World Trade Organization in 1995. The original 1947 GATT text is still in effect under the WTO framework, but has been modified by GATT 1994, the Final Act Embodying the Results of the Uruguay Round of Multilateral Trade Negotiations. In addition to the texts of the agreements, the Final Act also contains texts of Ministerial Decisions and Declarations which further clarify certain provisions of some of the agreements. GATT 1949 was negotiated during the 1944 UN Conference on Trade and Employment and was the outcome of the failure of negotiating governments to create the International Trade Organization (ITO).

2. World Trade Organization

The World Trade Organization (WTO) is the only global international organization dealing with the rules of trade between nations. The WTO agreements, negotiated and signed by most of the world's trading nations, are intended to supervise and liberalize international trade and assist producers of goods and services, exporters, and importers conduct their business.

B. Intellectual Property

1. World Intellectual Property Organization

The World Intellectual Property Organization (WIPO) is a specialized UN agency headquartered in Geneva, Switzerland that was established by the 1967 WIPO Convention. Its purpose is to develop a balanced and accessible intellectual property system that protects intellectual property globally. This protection is effected through cooperation among WIPO's 184 member states and with international organizations.

2. Copyright

Although most countries do not require copyright registration in order to enjoy copyright protection, registration can offer several benefits, such as proof of ownership. Many countries have bilateral copyright relations with one another, such that each country agrees to honor other countries' citizens' copyrights.

3. Patents and Trademarks

A patent or trademark registered in one country does not afford protection in other countries; patents and trademarks must be filed in each country where protection is sought.

a. Patent Cooperation Treaty

The Patent Cooperation Treaty (PCT) (1970), done at Washington, DC, has made the process of applying for patents and trademarks in various countries much easier. By filing one patent application with the U.S. Patent and Trademark Office (USPTO), U.S. applicants, for example, can simultaneously seek protection in up to 127 countries (as of 2005).

b. *Madrid System for Trademarks*

The Madrid system for the international registration of marks (Madrid System), established in 1891, functions under the Madrid Agreement Concerning the International Registration of Marks (Madrid Agreement) (1891) and the Madrid Protocol (1989). The Madrid System is administered by the International Bureau of WIPO located in Geneva, Switzerland.

The Madrid Agreement, revised at Brussels in 1900, at Washington in 1911, at The Hague in 1925, at London in 1934, at Nice in 1957, and at Stockholm in 1967, and amended in 1979, has been in operation for more than 110 years with 56 members. The Madrid Protocol, which entered into force in 2004 and currently has 85 members, introduced changes to the Madrid system that enhanced its usefulness to trademark owners. It makes it easier to file for trademark registration in multiple countries. By filing one trademark application, applicants may simultaneously seek trademark protection of in up to 66 countries.

XII. ALTERNATIVE DISPUTE RESOLUTION

States may choose from a wide range of mechanisms in resolving international disputes peacefully. We have already examined legal adjudication in international tribunals such as the ICJ or the ECJ. Now we turn to alternative dispute resolution. Nonbinding measures include negotiation, mediation, and conciliation. When these fail, states may take recourse to binding arbitration.

A. Negotiation

A state may engage in *ad hoc* negotiation when its leadership believes that the decision or action of another state threatens its well being or security. These may either be direct negotiations between the parties or indirect negotiations involving third parties, such as the UN secretary-general, through good offices. Negotiations are usually pursued through the diplomatic channels of foreign ministries and diplomats, through more formal commissions, or through international summits. The UN, through the GA or the SC, may recommend solutions or dispute resolution methods.

B. Mediation

Mediation, a more formal means of conflict resolution than negotiation, usually involves a neutral third party who hears both sides of the controversy and assists the parties in reaching a resolution by encouraging negotiations, providing them with additional channels of communication, or proposing solutions.

C. Conciliation

An even more formal tool is conciliation, whereby a permanent or *ad hoc* commission is set up to conduct an investigation and search for a set of settlement terms that would likely be accepted by both parties. The parties to conciliation are not, however, bound by the proposed settlement terms.

D. Arbitration

1. Introduction

Still more formal in the toolkit of dispute resolution is arbitration, where the parties in a conflict submit to an arbitral tribunal that hears all sides and comes to a binding decision. The parties decide the scope of the arbitral tribunal powers.

Arbitration can be used as a means of resolving disputes of both public international law (disputes between two states or between a state and citizens of another state) and private international law (disputes between private litigants from different countries). Although the decisions rendered in international arbitration are binding, the parties have a great deal of discretion in deciding whether to submit to arbitration, the forum in which the arbitration will take place, the body of law to be applied, and who will serve as the arbitrator or arbitrators.

2. Enforcement of international arbitral awards

Although the results of arbitration are generally binding, states may challenge arbitral awards. The losing party may commence proceedings in the national courts of the arbitral *situs* to set aside, vacate, or annul the arbitral award, while the prevailing party may commence proceedings in the same national courts to "confirm" the award. The prevailing party may also seek to "enforce" the award in the national courts of the arbitral *situs* or in a foreign court. The 1958 Convention on the Recognition and Enforcement of Foreign Arbitral Awards, which has been adopted by 142 of the 192 United Nations member states, is particularly key in this area in that it requires courts of contracting states to give effect to private agreements to arbitrate and to recognize and enforce arbitration awards made in other contracting states.

APPENDICES

GLOSSARY

A

Aggression Also known as a Crime against peace, it is a crime generally defined under customary international law and the Nuremberg Principles as the planning, preparation, initiation, or waging of any war in violation of international law, treaties, or agreements, including participation, conspiracy or complicity in the same (see Nuremberg Principles VI and VII). Because the crime of aggression has not been defined in the SICC, the ICC will not prosecute it until a precise definition has been adopted (art. 5.2 SICC).

Air law The body of laws concerning civil aviation. In its broadest sense, it may also refer to all law involving any use of the air, including but not limited to civil aviation. *Also known as* Aviation law.

Alien Tort Claims Act A section of the USC that grants the federal district courts original jurisdiction "of any civil action by an alien for a tort only, committed in violation of the law of nations or a treaty of the United States" (28 USC 1350). The statute allows suit to be brought in US federal court by aliens for torts committed outside of the US in violation of international law.

Antarctic Treaty System System of treaties comprised of the Antarctic Treaty and related agreements, including the Convention for the Conservation of Antarctic Marine Living Resources (1980) and the Protocol on Environmental Protection to the Antarctic Treaty (1991). The Antarctic Treaty, signed by 47 countries and entering into force in 1961, sets aside Antarctica as a scientific preserve free from weapons testing and other military activity and establishes freedom of scientific investigation on the continent.

Aviation law *See* Air law.

B

Baseline Line from which the seaward limits of a state's territorial sea and other maritime zones of jurisdiction (contiguous zone, exclusive economic zone, etc.) are measured. Normally, a sea baseline follows the Low-water line of a state's coast (art. 5 UNCLOS), but it may also be drawn from the low-water line of reefs in the case of islands situated on atolls or of islands having fringing reefs (art. 6 UNCLOS) or, in the case of coastlines that are deeply indented and cut into or having fringing islands, straight baselines joining appropriate points may be used (art. 7.1 UNCLOS).

C

Cabotage The exclusive right of a country to control the air traffic within its borders.

Conciliation Means of conflict resolution where a permanent or *ad hoc* commission is set up to conduct an investigation and search for a set of settlement terms that would likely be accepted by both parties. The parties to conciliation are not bound by the proposed settlement terms. *Compare* Mediation.

Continental shelf (*Geography*) Extended perimeter of each continent that is underwater by relatively shallow seas (known as shelf seas) and gulfs. (*Law*) Under UNCLOS, the continental shelf was legally defined as the stretch of the sea extending from the coast to the continental shelf.

Continental margin A steep continental slope followed by the flatter Continental rise.

Continental rise Pile of sediment that cascades down the slope and accumulates at the base of the continental slope. It is found between the continental slope and the abyssal plain.

Convention for the Protection of Human Rights and Fundamental Freedoms An international treaty to protect human rights and fundamental freedoms in Europe. It was drafted in 1950 by the then newly formed Council of Europe and entered into force in 1953. *Informally known as* EUROPEAN CONVENTION ON HUMAN RIGHTS.

Court An assembly, normally of a permanent nature, of one or more judges with the authority to judge on and adjudicate legal claims or disputes. Normally created by state law. *Compare* TRIBUNAL.

Crime against peace *See* AGGRESSION.

Crime of aggression *See* AGGRESSION.

Crimes against humanity Certain enumerated inhuman and odious acts committed as part of a systematic attack against any civilian population that constitute grave humiliation or degradation or a serious attack on human dignity. The SICC enumerates a series of crimes, including murder, extermination, and enslavement, that constitute crimes against humanity when "committed as part of a widespread or systematic attack directed against any civilian population, with knowledge of the attack" (art. 7.1 SICC).

Customary international law A source of international law consisting of (i) a consistent and recurrent state practice; (ii) developed over time; that is (iii) undertaken out of a sense of legal obligation. It thus results from a general and consistent practice of states followed by them from a sense of legal obligation.

D

Domestic law *See* MUNICIPAL LAW.

Draft Articles on the Responsibility of States for Internationally Wrongful Acts Non-binding declaration drafted by the ILC in 2001 that attempts to codify the rules under customary law for state responsibility. It serves as evidence of customary international law.

E

European Convention on Human Rights *See* CONVENTION FOR THE PROTECTION OF HUMAN RIGHTS AND FUNDAMENTAL FREEDOMS.

G

GATT *See* GENERAL AGREEMENT ON TARIFFS AND TRADE 1949 *and* GENERAL AGREEMENT ON TARIFFS AND TRADE 1994.

General Agreement on Tariffs and Trade (1949) An agreement negotiated during the UN Conference on Trade and Employment that was the outcome of the failure of negotiating governments to create the International Trade Organization (ITO). It was formed in 1949 and lasted until 1993. The World Trade Organization replaced it in 1995. *Known by its acronym* GATT. *See also* GENERAL AGREEMENT ON TARIFFS AND TRADE (1994).

General Agreement on Tariffs and Trade (1994) The Final Act Embodying the Results of the Uruguay Round of Multilateral Trade Negotiations, signed by ministers in Marrakesh in 1994. In addition to the texts of the agreements, the Final Act also contains texts of Ministerial Decisions and Declarations which further clarify certain provisions of some of the agreements. The original 1947 GATT text is still in effect under the WTO system, subject to modifications under the 1994 GATT text. *See also* GENERAL AGREEMENT ON TARIFFS AND TRADE (1949).

General principle of law A source of international law that serves as a gap filler by international courts when there is no applicable treaty provision or rule of customary international law. The court will try to ascertain general principles of law by finding commonalities among well-development legal systems in the world. These general principles may include both principles of law and principles of equity.

Genocide Defined under the Genocide Convention and the SICC as any of the following acts committed on members of any national, ethnical, religious or racial group with the intent to destroy it: killing, causing of serious bodily or mental harm, prevention of birth, transferring of children to another group, or infliction of conditions of life calculated to bring about its physical destruction (art. II CPPG; art. 6 SICC).

Grotius (Hugo) Dutch jurist whose writings established the basis of modern international law. In his treatise *De jure belli ac pacis libri tres* (*On the Law of War and Peace: Three books*), he advances a system of principles of natural law that he holds to be binding on all people and nations regardless of local custom, and then goes on to outline the circumstances under which war may be justly executed.

H

Hague Conference on Private International Law Preeminent organization in private international law formed in 1893 to work for the progressive unification of the rules of private international law by assisting in the implementation of multilateral conventions promoting the harmonization of conflict of laws principles. Sixty-eight nations, including China, Russia, the United States, and all of the EU countries, are currently members.

House of Lords The UK's final appeals court.

Human Rights Committee HUMAN RIGHTS TREATY BODY of the International Covenant on Civil and Political Rights (ICCPR). It has power to: (i) elaborate on the norms in the ICCPR; and (ii) hear complaints from individuals against states.

Human rights treaty body Committee of independent experts charged with monitoring the implementation of an international human rights treaty and considering individual complaints or communications. Human rights treaty bodies are created by the human rights treaties that they implement.

I

Inland waters Lakes, rivers, and ports located within the boundaries of a state. States are fully sovereign over their inland waters and may enforce their laws in full against foreign marine ships.

International Committee of the Red Cross Impartial private humanitarian organization based in Geneva, Switzerland that works to protect the victims of international and domestic armed conflicts. Its mandate stems from the four Geneva Conventions of 1949 and states parties to the Conventions and their Protocols Additional of 1977 and 2005 have given the ICRC a mandate to protect the victims of war and armed violence.

International crime Internationally wrongful act resulting from the breach by a state, state agent, or non-state actor of a peremptory norm (*jus cogens*) so essential for the protection of the international community's fundamental interests that its breach is classified by the community as a crime (*e.g.*, aggression, torture, genocide).

International humanitarian law Set of rules regulating the conduct of war and armed hostilities. These rules restrict the means and methods of warfare and seek to limit the effects of armed conflict for humanitarian reasons by protecting civilians who are not or are no longer participating in the hostilities. *Also known as* LAW OF WAR, LAW OF ARMED CONFLICT, and *JUS IN BELLO*. *Compare* JUS AD BELLUM.

International Law Commission A commission established by the UN General Assembly in 1948 for the "promotion of the progressive development of international law and its codification" (art. 1 of the ILC Statute). It has held sessions in Geneva every year since 1949 that have lead to the creation of the Vienna Convention on the Law of Treaties, the Vienna Convention on Diplomatic Relations, and the Draft Articles on the Responsibility of States for Internationally Wrongful Acts, among others.

International Law Institute A private, non-for-profit organization chartered by Georgetown University that conducts scholarly research, publishing, and practical legal training and technical assistance in order to promote economic development and rule of law and address the challenges faced by the international community.

International organization A body created by a treaty with a permanent institutional structure whose membership consists either exclusively or in large part of states. The treaty is the constituent instrument of the organization.

International seabed area Portion of the sea that lies beyond the limits of national jurisdiction, underlying most of the world's oceans.

International uniform law Refers to the situation whereby the domestic laws of nations have been made uniform by agreement.

J

Jus ad bellum (*Lat.*, "Justice in the resort to war") Laws that regulate recourse to the use of armed force. *Compare* JUS IN BELLO.

Jus Cogens (*Lat.*) *See* PEREMPTORY NORM OF GENERAL INTERNATIONAL LAW.

Jus in bello (*Lat.*, "Justice in the conduct of war") *See* International humanitarian law. *Compare* Jus ad bellum.

L

Law of armed conflict *See* INTERNATIONAL HUMANITARIAN LAW.

Law of Nations Name given in the past to refer to international law.

Law of war *See* INTERNATIONAL HUMANITARIAN LAW.

Low-water line The location of the coastline at low tide. *Also known as* LOW-WATER MARK.

Low-water mark *See* LOW-WATER LINE.

M

Mediation Means of conflict resolution that usually involves a neutral third party who hears both sides of a controversy and assists the parties in reaching a resolution by encouraging negotiations, providing the parties with additional channels of communication, or proposing solutions. The parties to conciliation are not bound by proposed settlement terms. *Compare* CONCILIATION.

Municipal law For the purposes of international law, municipal law is the internal law that applies within a country. *Also known as* DOMESTIC LAW *or* NATIONAL LAW.

N

National law *See* MUNICIPAL LAW.

North Atlantic Treaty Treaty that created the NORTH ATLANTIC TREATY ORGANIZATION.

North Atlantic Treaty Organization Alliance of 26 countries from North America and Europe committed to fulfilling the goals of the NORTH ATLANTIC TREATY.

Nuremberg Principles Text drafted by the ILC in response to the UN GA's 1950 request to formulate the principles of international law recognized in the Charter of the IMT and in the judgment of the Tribunal. Formally known as the "Principles of International Law Recognized in the Charter of the Nüremberg Tribunal and in the Judgment of the Tribunal."

O

Organisation of African Unity (OAU) Established in 1963 to promote the unity and solidarity of the African states and act as a collective voice for Africa and to eradicate all forms of colonialism. Dissolved in 2002 and replaced by the AU.

Opinio juris (*Lat.*) A source of international law comprised of "the judicial decisions and the teachings of the most highly qualified publicists of the various nations" (art. 38 SICJ). *Opinio juris* may be comprised of not only judicial decisions and the writings of judges, scholars, and other experts, but also of the resolutions and declarations of international organizations.

P

Pacta sunt servanda (*Lat.*) "Agreements must be kept."

Peace of Westphalia Series of peace treaties signed in 1648 in Osnabrück and Münster, Germany, that ended the Thirty Years' War (1618–1648) in the Holy Roman Empire and the Eighty Years' War (1568–1648) between Spain and the Dutch Republic.

Peremptory norm of general international law Norm accepted and recognized by the international community as a norm from which no derogation is permitted and which can be modified only by a subsequent norm of general international law having the same character (art. 53 VCLT). Examples include prohibitions on torture, slavery, genocide, and aggression. *Also known as* JUS COGENS.

Propio motu (*Lat.*) By one's own volition.

Protocol Subsidiary agreement built from a primary treaty, often implementing or applying the primary treaty, incorporating recent political or scientific developments. They often permit countries to enter into agreement by signing a general framework and to later work out details as to implementation via protocols.

R

Right to innocent passage The right to sail in territorial seas as long as the sailing is not prejudicial to the peace of the coastal state.

S

Sic utere (*Lat.*) General principle of good neighborliness in environmental law, from the Latin expression *sic utere tuo ut alienum non laedas* ("so use your own as not to injure another's property").

Special drawing right International reserve asset created by the IMF to supplement member countries' official reserves. Its value is based on four key international currencies and it can be exchanged for freely usable currencies. There are at present 204 billion SDRs (approx. $308 billion) at the time of writing.

State actor An actor for whose conduct a nexus to state action may be established.

Strafe Attack with machine guns or cannon fire from a low-flying plane.

T

Terra nullius (*Lat.*, "the land of no one") Land that is not under the sovereignty or control of any state. States may obtain title to *terra nullius* through the occupation thereof.

Tribunal An assembly, usually of an *ad hoc* nature, of one or more judges with the authority to judge on and adjudicate legal claims or disputes. *Compare* COURT.

U

UNCITRAL A UN body charged with promoting the harmonization of international trade law and regulating international trade in cooperation with the WORLD TRADE ORGANIZATION.

UNIDROIT Independent intergovernmental organization with 59 member states whose purpose is to examine ways of harmonizing, modernizing and coordinating the domestic private law of states and in particular commercial law. The organization, seated in Rome, is neither a UN body nor a UN agency.

United Nations Commission on Human Rights UN commission that in 2006 was replaced by the UNITED NATIONS HUMAN RIGHTS COUNCIL. It was a subsidiary body of ECOSOC concerned with drafting human rights treaties for adoption by the UN GA, and was also assisted in its work by the UNHCHR as the UN's principal mechanism and international forum concerned with the promotion and protection of human rights.

United Nations Human Rights Council Successor to the UNITED NATIONS COMMISSION ON HUMAN RIGHTS. As a subsidiary body of the UN General Assembly, it is responsible for strengthening the promotion and protection of human rights around the globe. The Council was created by the UN General Assembly on 15 March 2006 with the main purpose of addressing situations of human rights violations and making recommendations on them.

Universal jurisdiction Jurisdiction that applies to the most egregious of crimes, such as genocide, and allows the courts of any nation to try nationals of any other nation without the consent of the latter nation. This is an exception to the general rule that sovereign nations may only be sued when they waive immunity.

Uti possidetis (*Lat.*, "as you possess") International legal principle that holds that territory and other property possessed at the end of a conflict remains with the possessor, unless otherwise provided for by treaty. This principle enables a belligerent party to legitimately claim territory that it has acquired by war.

W

War crime Defined by the Geneva Conventions as a criminal violation or grave breach of INTERNATIONAL HUMANITARIAN LAW (the law of war). The London Charter gave the following examples of war crimes under the jurisdiction of the IMT: "murder, ill-treatment or deportation to slave labor or for any other purpose of civilian population of or in occupied territory, murder or ill-treatment of prisoners of war or persons on the seas, killing of hostages, plunder of public or private property, wanton destruction of cities, towns or villages, or devastation not justified by military necessity" (art. 6(b) IMT). The SICC includes a more extensive list in its eighth article.

WIPO (World Intellectual Property Organization)

WTO (World Trade Organization) The only global international organization dealing with the rules of trade between nations. The WTO agreements, negotiated and signed by most of the world's trading nations, are intended to supervise and liberalize international trade and assist producers of goods and services, exporters, and importers conduct their business.

CHARTS AND GRAPHS

Common Articles 2 and 3 of the 1949 Geneva Conventions

Article	Content
Common Article 2 (for international conflicts)	In addition to the provisions which shall be implemented in peace-time, the present Convention shall apply to all cases of declared war or of any other armed conflict which may arise between two or more of the High Contracting Parties, even if the state of war is not recognized by one of them. The Convention shall also apply to all cases of partial or total occupation of the territory of a High Contracting Party, even if the said occupation meets with no armed resistance. Although one of the Powers in conflict may not be a party to the present Convention, the Powers who are parties thereto shall remain bound by it in their mutual relations. They shall furthermore be bound by the Convention in relation to the said Power, if the latter accepts and applies the provisions thereof.
Common Article 3 (for internal conflicts)	In the case of armed conflict not of an international character occurring in the territory of one of the High Contracting Parties, each Party to the conflict shall be bound to apply, as a minimum, the following provisions: (1) Persons taking no active part in the hostilities, including members of armed forces who have laid down their arms and those placed *hors de combat* by sickness, wounds, detention, or any other cause, shall in all circumstances be treated humanely, without any adverse distinction founded on race, colour, religion or faith, sex, birth or wealth, or any other similar criteria. To this end the following acts are and shall remain prohibited at any time and in any place whatsoever with respect to the above-mentioned persons: (a) violence to life and person, in particular murder of all kinds, mutilation, cruel treatment and torture; (b) taking of hostages; (c) outrages upon personal dignity, in particular humiliating and degrading treatment; (d) the passing of sentences and the carrying out of executions without previous judgment pronounced by a regularly constituted court, affording all the judicial guarantees which are recognized as indispensable by civilized peoples. (2) The wounded and sick shall be collected and cared for. An impartial humanitarian body, such as the International Committee of the Red Cross, may offer its services to the Parties to the conflict. The Parties to the conflict should further endeavour to bring into force, by means of special agreements, all or part of the other provisions of the present Convention.

	The application of the preceding provisions shall not affect the legal status of the Parties to the conflict.

Geneva Conventions: Overview

Convention	Revising	Function
Convention (I) for the Amelioration of the Condition of the Wounded and Sick in Armed Forces in the Field. Geneva, 1949 Original: 1864	The Geneva Convention for the Relief of the Wounded and Sick in Armies in the Field of July 27, 1929 First Geneva Convention (1864)	- Protects wounded and sick soldiers on land during war; - Protects medical and religious personnel, medical units, and medical transports. - Contains a draft agreement relating to hospital zones and a model identity card for medical and religious personnel.
Convention (II) for the Amelioration of the Condition of Wounded, Sick and Shipwrecked Members of Armed Forces at Sea. Geneva, 1949 Original 1906	Xth Hague Convention of October 18, 1907 for the Adaptation to Maritime Warfare of the Principles of the Geneva Convention of 1906	- Protects wounded, sick and shipwrecked military personnel at sea during war at sea.
Convention (III) relative to the Treatment of Prisoners of War. Geneva, 1949 Original: 1929	Convention concluded at Geneva on July 27, 1929, relative to the Treatment of Prisoners of War	- Applies to prisoners of war. - Established the principle of repatriating prisoners of war immediately upon the cessation of hostilities.
Convention (IV) relative to the Protection of Civilian Persons in Time of War. Geneva, 1949 Original: 1949	NA	- Protects civilians, including those in occupied territories. - Outlines the rights of those captured during military conflicts; - Protects the wounded and civilians in war zones.

Maritime Zones of Jurisdiction

Category	Geography	Rights of Coastal State
High Seas	Beyond the continental shelf, in the deep seabed.	- Ships are subject to international law and the law of state. - The right of hot pursuit for violations of its laws if the pursuit began in its internal or archipelagic waters, territorial sea, or contiguous zones and is uninterrupted.
Continental Shelf	Based on geology survey, but no more than 350 miles	- Sovereign exclusive rights for exploring it and exploiting its natural resources (mineral and other non-living resources and living *sedentary* organisms)

	from baselines or 100 miles from 2,500 meter isobath	
Exclusive Economic Zone	Up to 200 miles from baselines	- Exclusive rights to fish, exploit biological resources, mine minerals from and exploit the seabed, produce energy from the currents and wind, etc.
Contiguous Zone	Up to 24 miles from baselines	- Jurisdiction for enforcing customs, fiscal, sanitary, and immigration laws and punishing infringements thereof. - Exclusive rights to fish, exploit biological resources, mine minerals from and exploit the seabed, produce energy from the currents and wind, etc.
Territorial Sea	Up to 12 miles from baselines	- Coastal state may enforce its criminal jurisdiction. - Jurisdiction for enforcing customs, fiscal, sanitary, and immigration laws and punishing infringements thereof. - Exclusive rights to regulate airspace above. - Exclusive rights to fish, exploit biological resources, mine minerals from and exploit the seabed, produce energy from the currents and wind, etc.
Internal waters	Inland lakes, rivers, and ports	- Territorial sovereignty. - Coastal state may enforce its civil and criminal jurisdiction. - Jurisdiction for enforcing customs, fiscal, sanitary, and immigration laws and punishing infringements thereof. - Exclusive rights to regulate airspace above - Exclusive rights to fish, exploit biological resources, mine minerals from and exploit the seabed, produce energy from the currents and wind, etc.

Public verses Private International Law

Question or Scenario	Public	Private
Rights between several nations	✓	
Human rights abuse by a state of an individual person	✓	
Expropriation by a state of the property of an alien corporation	✓[2]	
Activities of and relations between natural and juridical persons when they cross national borders when governed by domestic conflict of laws provisions.		✓

Public International Law versus Conflict of Laws

Organization	What it Does	Category

---

[2] Assuming that the alien sues the expropriating state under an international legal provision, such as a treaty, the case would fall under public international law. However, if he sues under the state's domestic alien tort statutes, the case would fall under private international law.

HCPIL	Harmonizes domestic rules for conflict of laws. Concluded 36 multilateral treaties.	Private international law
UNIDROIT	Harmonize states' substantive domestic laws, especially commercial.	Private international law
UNCITRAL	Harmonizes international trade law.	Private international law
WTO	Supervises and liberalizes international trade through agreements negotiated and signed by trading nations.	Public international law